AF862655

ON THE SOCIOLOGY OF INTERNATIONAL LAW AND INTERNATIONAL SOCIETY

ON THE SOCIOLOGY OF INTERNATIONAL LAW AND INTERNATIONAL SOCIETY

by

BART LANDHEER

Director, Peace Palace Library, The Hague
Special Professor of the Sociology of International Relations, University of Groningen, Netherlands

MARTINUS NIJHOFF / THE HAGUE / 1966

ISBN 978-94-015-0268-9 ISBN 978-94-015-0792-9 (eBook)
DOI 10.1007/978-94-015-0792-9

Copyright 1966 by Martinus Nijhoff, The Hague, Netherlands
All rights reserved, including the right to translate or to reproduce this book or parts thereof in any form

TABLE OF CONTENTS

PREFACE

The academic or scientific occupation with international relations is not always an encouraging task. At times one gets an image of the enormous psychic and physical forces which operate in the international realm, and it then seems that the role of the publicist is almost a negligible one. If one, in addition, arrives at the conclusion that human social action is not really a volitional process, then there is indeed ample room for pessimism and despair.

Nevertheless, in the complexity of our consciousness, the different elements of which life is made of blend into a unity of which the idea is as much a part or even more so than the deed or action. The stress on action expresses the crudeness of our times but the idea has been much more the motivation of history and its cohesive force over long periods. Action in terms of force is never in itself the entire solution because it carries no conviction or understanding, at least unless its role is a very moderate one.

It is the mentality with which we approach life which determines to a large extent its reality. It is one of the strange beliefs of modern society that life should be made "scientific" or conducted "scientifically" in order to be satisfactory. If this were so, this would imply that scientific Man as the new form of homo sapiens is the Man of the Future. Even if this were so, the question remains what type of knowledge we need. Certainly not technical knowledge because this seems to have run to full cycle of its usefulness so that there could be only question of a knowledge of Man and of his social interrelationships. If this knowledge is the essential one, we cannot separate it into a knowledge of international relations, of national societies and of the individual unless there is some basic philosophy in which these three perspectives find their roots and whence they take their inspiration.

It is basically our image of Man which determines these approaches, but unfortunately, this image is far from clear. Man knows himself and the world around him only as a function of his consciousness, and the analysis of the structure of his consciousness is the only possible starting-point for an ordered occupation with his behaviour.

The consciousness of the individual reflects that part of the world which is "his world", and not anything like Mankind, the nation, science or anything which can be adequately represented by an abstract term. The reference to "the others" in abstract terms is mostly a device by which it is sought to influence people.

It is exactly this factor of people influencing other people which obscures our thinking and makes it impossible for many of us to know and formulate what we want ourselves. Nevertheless, this is the only possibility because if we continue to attribute qualities to the individual which he does not really possess, chaos is close at hand because meaningful communication between human beings will disappear and be replaced by shadowy verbal behaviour which has little or no reality.

Nevertheless, it is not possible to return to the individualism of past periods because Man is only alive in intercommunication with his natural and social surroundings. He needs this reality, but not the patterns of consciousness which do not reflect his own interests, but those of others.

If we would let social growth take its course, an intricate network of social relationships would result in which there would be no longer many forms of authoritative leadership. Man only accepts this when there is a need for it, and this need has largely disappeared from our world. We have become bewildered, however, by the success of our control over nature, and we attempt to transfer those controls to the manipulation of human beings. This overlooks, however, the most basic attribute of human life: the control over nature was a legitimate goal because Man rejected emotionally the system of scarcity under which he had lived for many centuries. He does not accept emotionally any authoritative or scientific social control-systems which would annul the freedom which he seeks even more than material well-being. It is this sense of freedom which must be reestablished: the freedom of politics; economic freedom; the freedom of privacy; the freedom to seek those social forms which correspond to the volition of the individual; the freedom to engage in those activities which are emotionally rewarding to us. It does not matter whether they fit into any plan.

Man may be able to plan much, but he has not planned himself. The way he is structured, he can only live if he strives for balance, continuity and happiness. It is not scientific Man who will create the future, but simply Man with his emotions, passions and frustrations which will be forever with us, but instead of manipulating them, we should seek to guide and restrain them.

Seen in this way international relations are nothing more than one aspect of the eternal problem of interhuman problems, and in this way they have been dealt with in this brief study.

BART LANDHEER

CHAPTER I

INTRODUCTION

The complexity of our sciences reflects the complexity of our society, and it is no wonder, as international problems loom larger in our thinking, that the scientific approach to these problems has also become far more complex than in the past.

Originally, in the thinking of Antiquity, it was largely history which occupied itself with the events involving more than one national group or city-state to which one could add social philosophy, religion and law which dealt with problems like war and peace, ambassadors, treaties, etc. As mostly one state or group of states occupied a dominant position, international problems were viewed as a specific aspect of national problems.

The Romans in particular thought in terms of the Roman Empire, though in the philosophy of the stoics we find ideas about the universal brotherhood of Man and about a world-state. The Middle Ages established a firm ethical basis for human behaviour, but Christian ethics did not distinguish between nationals and foreigners, but only between Christians and Non-Christians. Consequently, one should not add "ethics" to the sciences which occupied themselves with international problems, at least not for the period to which we are referring. Nevertheless, in the gradual evolvement of the concepts of natural law, we find the beginnings of what was going to be termed "international law," after the national states of Western Europe had become the dominant social groups.

It was the New Era which brought the appearance of international law, seen very definitely by its originator Hugo Grotius as a means of establishing order among the nations and of restricting war as far as possible. To Grotius law was to be a motive rather than a technique in international action so that there was no clear dividing line between natural law and international law, but the latter discipline gradually separated itself from the former.

After history, social philosophy and law, it was economics which brought international problems within its ken, as in the period of Mercantilism, while politics became a science ever since the days of Machiavelli's "The Prince," though its fuller flowering came only in the nineteenth century.

As international relations were first and foremost relations between nations via their governments, history, international law and diplomacy retained a firm hold on the study of international problems, though economics pursued its own trends of thinking.

The twentieth century brought, however, several new phenomena which could not be brought entirely within the orbit of the existing sciences, like the ideological movements which created new types of civilisations. Western civilisation gradually became a civilisation alongside – instead of above – a number of civilisations, and this makes it essential for us to rethink our problems, and particularly our international ones, within a new setting. They can no longer be viewed from a national viewpoint or from the viewpoint of a specific civilisation if we are aiming for a coordinated world.

This process of re-thinking can obviously never be the prerogative of one specific science, but it could be claimed that the sociological approach has certain specific advantages.

The reasons for this are the following: in the first place, sociology emerged in Western society when individualism and rationalism had passed their peak and when Western society was seeking greater unity and a better equilibrium within the nation-states though not as yet between them. Excessive individualism had undermined the cohesion of society while rationalism had proved itself to be a too one-sided philosophy. Man was definitely not a predominantly rational creature as the nineteenth as well as the twentieth century proved beyond any shadow of doubt.

When sociology arose as a separate science, it therefore identified itself with the efforts to see the group rather than the individual and to test progress in terms of definite human goals instead of as the vague general philosophy of a dynamic society.

There is a certain parallel between the problems of the national societies of the nineteenth and early twentieth century and of world society of today. In both cases we find excessive individualism, not in terms of classes within national societies, but in terms of nationalism, while we find also excessive social distance between the under-developed and the developed nations, just like that existing between the classes of the nineteenth century.

This similarity certainly does not mean the two situations are identical: classes are not nations though nations in our period cast themselves in this role by using class-philosophies. National superiorities and inferiorities are not the same as class-superiority. Nevertheless, we deal with these phenomena in terms of groups, and in this respect sociology has had the experience of dealing with comparable group problems, though in a different setting. In this respect, it holds a certain advantage over psychology which takes its starting point in the individual.

Furthermore, sociology has devoted great attention to social change while legal thinking has an innate static trend. In world society, however, change plays a dominant role, and this role must find its expression in our thinking about world-society. It is a particularly pressing task to find a certain link between the idea of equilibrium and that of change, because on the surface they seem to exclude one another, and this could have the most disastrous results for world society.

In sociology it has become customary to distinguish between universal social theories and middle or short-range theories. From the empirical viewpoint that prevails particularly in the United States, there is a marked preference for the middle and short-range theories which are also of value for international situations, such as those concerning ethnic conflicts, adjustment to culture-change, etc. While it cannot be denied that general social theories easily contain a speculative element, there is nevertheless a great need for a general theory of international society, and in this respect the early systems of sociological thinking of Comte, Spencer and others offer a useful starting point.

A theory of world society is in a way a vision on world society, and as long as this vision is realistic, it can be accepted that it could not possibly be empirical. An empirical vision is a contradiction in terms, but in spite of this we must strive for a global perspective in our thinking if we want to break through ideological and nationalistic forms of thought. Even the sciences of Western society are not free from prejudice, and it is a wrong starting-point to assume that they can furnish solutions for the world as a whole.

The world as a whole has to be heard, and no part of it should impute its thinking to all of mankind.

It is particularly in the sociology of knowledge that attempts have been made to investigate the relationship between socio-economic patterns and patterns of thought. This relationship is of crucial importance because one third of mankind has a definite theory about it which is not shared by the other two thirds. But a simple denial is not a constructive contribution: this relationship should be seen in its great complexity, and not in terms of any direct interdependence.

The abstract idea of the rational and independent individual has been replaced in sociology by that of the structured group of which the individual forms a part. This idea of structure is of great importance to the study of world society because it counteracts the fictitious idea of "self-determination."

In contemporary world society there is no "self-determination" because every action of state A influences states B, C, D, etc. We may use fictions in international thinking as is done in law, but we must be aware that we are dealing with fictions rather than realities.

And we must raise the question whether these fictions are still useful. Our thinking about international problems is largely in terms of the nineteenth century, and, while this neither confirms, nor condemns a term or a concept, it is at least a very sound reason for re-examination of the terminology in question which is applied to totally different situations.

In order to remedy this situation, there is even place for the attempts to analyse international problems in diagrammatic and even in mathematical language. It may be confusing, but it is at least a new type of confusion, compared to an old one which has the disadvantage of being regarded as realistic.

"Real" are only individuals, and the ultimate approach to international problems lies in the motivation and identification of individuals. We have many roles: in small groups like the family, our professional role, our role as a citizen, our role as a member of an ideological group or a civilisation or a religious group, finally our role as a member of world society.

How do we combine these roles and what causes the domination, sometimes quite suddenly, of one role over many others? These questions are very startling ones, and even if we could solve them in theory, we cannot solve them in practice, unless those in power so desire.

Clear thinking can lead, however, to responsible action while the chances are definitely small that unclear thinking by accident could lead to responsible action. At any rate, we should not want to build world society upon such a flimsy foundation.

Thus clear, analytical and constructive thinking has its place in our efforts to find a solution for world society, even though these forms of thinking can be no more than a small contribution. It is perhaps better to realize this than to strive for theoretical recipes which are either ignored or revised a few years later.

This is not to deny the desirability of a theory of international relations or of international society, but rather to state a postulate in its own right rather than for its practical consequences which depend upon the volition of others. Even if we could prove mathematically that a certain course of action would lead to disaster, this course might still be chosen by the political decision-makers.

The opposite is equally or even more possible, and this alternative does not diminish the value of theory.

Whether the theoretical approach to international problems should make a fresh start as is claimed by the theorists of international relations or whether it can find its starting point in an existing science seems a moot question. Economics separated from moral and legal philosophy and gradually became a science of its own because it created a specific perspective plus a solid mass of social facts that were regarded as predominantly economic.

The perspective is the essential factor because the social facts are always more simple than our thinking about them.

In other words, what we need first and foremost is a global perspective, and it is with this task that this study will deal, taking its starting point in our present forms of thinking and attempting to analyse what changes might be needed if we really strive for a coordinated world society. Of course, if this motive is not genuine and real in enough people, no theories or books can create such a society, just like law-books and statutes do not create law-abiding citizens.

But once the motive is present, tentative formulations can become of value, and we should at least start by assuming that the will for a functioning world society lives in most of us.

CHAPTER II

THE BASIS OF AND REASON FOR A SOCIOLOGICAL APPROACH

If we consider the creation of global forms of thinking as the most important task of the sociology of international society, we have first to ask ourselves in what way we can arrive at such forms of thought upon a sociological basis. Global forms of thought exist in terms of world religions and general ideologies while international law regards itself as the science which occupies itself with the ordering of international society.

The world religions and ideologies have become identified in our time mostly with specific areas, and to some extent they can be regarded as parts of regional value-systems, though this obviously does not mean that they are not directing themselves at people all over the world, but these influences have become weaker than in preceding systems as most contemporary culture-systems have the tendency to restrict rather severely the propagation of other value-systems. This has also resulted in there being little or no international discussion of these value-systems, as they consist more of absolute social values than of intellectual ones which can be tested and evaluated. This means that there can be no global philosophy unless some compromise is reached between these near absolute value-systems.

In global communication, the states use international law as a technique of communication, though its values are by no means to be found in all the regional value-systems. This has resulted in the custom of seeing international law as a system of means which can be adjusted to specific purposes, but the values of international law are but rarely motives as such for international action. Whether this is due to a weakness of international law as a value-system or to its limited rate of efficacy is a problem that needs further elaboration.

For the moment we may accept the conclusion that it is not at present a universal value-system, perhaps partially because it still accepts the state as the actor in international society, and neither the individual nor the regional group have a strong place in international law, while it is also not as yet equipped to incorporate the concept of change into its system.

This absence of universal values is a very serious hindrance to the emergence of a world society, and it can never be the task of a science to create such values which must come forth from life itself. A science which strives for objectivity can, however, describe the various value-systems and place them in their historical setting while it can also investigate the social functions of these values rather than accept them as such.

The coexistence of value-systems is in itself the reflection of actually existing divisions in world-society, and it should be observed that the development towards culture-groups consisting of a large state or of a combination of states is in itself an advantage over the preceding period which knew only the individual state as the dominant factor in world society. While there are still but very few signs of an emerging world society, we have witnessed the appearance of groups of states which pursue related goals, and this development could form the transitional stage towards a world society.

At any rate one must begin with the reality of these groups, and no investigation of international problems can be fruitful unless it starts upon the basis of a world divided into a Western and a Communist bloc, groups like the Arab States or those of Latin America, the emerging federations in Europe and Africa and the larger uncommitted nations, of which India is the dominant example. The fact which stands out is the emergence of large social groups, consisting of a dominant state with satellites or allies, as this form did not exist in the preceding period.

These large-group societies are the only ones which can use modern technology effectively, and one could say that our social forms have indeed reacted to technical developments, though it is customary to speak about a "lag" between technology and social organisation. The modern highly complex large-group society is, however, only possible upon the basis of modern technology, and any comparison with social groups like the states of the nineteenth century is in reality entirely misleading. One could even go further and say that the difference in the value-systems of the two dominant societies is largely due to the different way and the different period in which they incorporated the emergence of modern industry into their value-systems. They both regard modern industry as the key to power, and a good deal of the difference lies in the tension between already existing power and projected power, which obviously demand different social values and different social techniques.

Communism originated as a class ideology destined to overcome the status lag of the working class, and this ideology, though not without significant changes, has become the national ideology of countries which show a particular sensitivity of their status lag in world society.

One can notice this again in the case of China, which adheres to the most radical form of communism, partially because it had the greatest lag between actual and projected status.

Nevertheless, in so far as there is a universal global philosophy, this philosophy proclaims its belief in an egalitarian world society and it shows considerable concern about remedying the status-lag of various parts of the world. In theory there seems to be no reason why development aided by others should be preferable to self-help, though one could suppose that self-help is a kind of uncontrolled social motion from the viewpoint of the maintenance of the status quo.

The world of the nineteen hundred sixties cannot be regarded in terms of an equilibrium, but only in terms of the possibilities of an equilibrium which is fostered or hampered by actual events. The possibilities of an equilibrium do not lie so much, however, in the coexistence of a hundred states as in the coexistence, which gradually would have to become a structured one, of the different regional groups which have become already visible.

Since nineteen hundred and ten there has been a great structural change in our world which has been reflected in and influenced by our thinking. Now the problem is how to foresee further developments and to ascertain what modes of thinking would be appropriate for them.

Roughly speaking, only three alternatives exist:

1. The present tensions leading to a conflict out of which only one major power or chaos emerges.

2. The organisation of the world in terms of the emerging power-structure, with due provisions for reasonable and peaceful change.

3. The organisation of the world in terms of a hundred, legally equal states with an international superstructure. This is more or less the nineteenth century recipe, though the nineteenth century itself showed a totally different structure of world society.

Strategic bloc-thinking is the form which corresponds to situation 1 and possibly 2. It must be added, however, that status-quo bloc-thinking has no clear image of the future, and the status quo idea can never be more than a temporary solution as it does not envisage a functioning world society which has to aim at coordination rather than co-existence.

Alternative 3 still plays a large role in legal thinking and in international organisation, though it is widely realised that it is too formalistic and too static. It also does not provide a bridge to a coordinated world society, except in terms of a legalistic and egalitarian world government.

The differences in power between the hundred states are much too large, however, to make this development probable, while this approach also ignores the already existing trends towards bloc and regional developments.

Thus, the second alternative becomes the one which appears most feasible, and for this solution the sociological mode of thinking seems most adapted, because it views reality as such and not in terms of projected situations, while it would also support the idea that the emerging world society will have to create a superstructure of its own, with its own modes of thinking, and its own organisational forms. Needless to say these modes of thinking will also find a legal expression, but, first and foremost, there is a need for changes in the general forms of thought about world society.

One of the most remarkable aspects of international problems lies in the dualism of our thinking. We have one set of values by which we regulate our behavior in regard to the national society to which we belong while, in many cases, these values become almost reversed if we deal with international situations. We never deal with our neighbors as countries do, and yet the man who is our neighbor may be the one who is a decision-maker in international affairs. It is he who has the double values, not an abstract entity like the state.

The reason why there is a double value-system must largely be explained historically. Mankind does not develop evenly, but in expanding groups which come in contact with other groups, the more so as the space for expansion shrinks. The individual, however, identifies himself only with group A and not with group B. For this reason his ingroup-values are different from his outgroup-values, and he cannot overcome this dualism, unless values are purposely introduced which correspond to the interests of A + B as a coordinated group.

The will for coordination must precede the (A + B) values as these values can only become motives if they represent shared interests. The difficulty in world society is that there is no willingness to arrive at shared interests so that internationalism, international law, etc. remain verbal manifestations if they do not cover common interests. This limits international law to the common interests of the large powers as has been pointed out repeatedly.

Although situations are never identical, there is a certain similarity in these problems whether they refer to small or large groups.

The situation discussed above prevailed to a certain extent among the nation-states of the nineteenth century; now it prevails between the two dominant power-blocs and between nation-states, though influenced by power-bloc pressures. The realm of common interests was in some respects larger in the nineteenth century than in the twentieth century unless one wishes to regard the fear of thermo-nuclear war as a common interest.

Whether fear as a common emotion also constitutes a common interest is a difficult psychological problem. Fear of a common enemy unites; fear of one another divides. The present fear of thermo-nuclear war is not the fear of a technical development because if it were commonly held as an individual emotion in regard to a technical device, nothing would be easier than to drop it, as was the case with germ warfare when that did not become a reality.

But in reality we cannot speak of the fear of a technical device, but we must see this fear predominantly as the fear of the two blocs for one another.

This also accounts for the fact that disarmament discussions show very few results. It is much more essential to establish general common interests before means-to-ends problems can gain significance. Armaments are a means-to-an-end, and not ends in themselves, though in our complex society they also gain that quality by being regarded as economic catalysts.

Other economic solutions, however, are certainly not impossible, and it remains justified to say that the main cause of continued international friction lies in the fact that the area of common interests is too small, smaller even than in the period of dominance of the European nation-states.

In that period, there were many common interests: common religious and humanitarian values, a certain belief in the validity of international law, many cultural interests, common professional and economic interests, etc. As we can never separate human activities from their carriers, one can point to the churches which were more international than national; one can point to the nobility, and to the world of learning and literature; one can point to vast trans-national economic interests.

In the East-West situation the situation is much more negative because there are very few carriers of trans-bloc activities; there is no interaction on the ideological level but there are some contacts via international organisations; there is some cultural exchange, some tourism and some commerce, but if one were to evaluate these contacts in terms of their carriers, one would arrive at a very small percentage compared to, for instance, French-German contacts before 1914.

One could remark that contacts alone do not establish a realm of common interests. They can also intensify conflicts and antagonism. This is undoubtedly true, but a lack of contacts means that the social growth of the different entities takes place largely independently, and it is very hard to see how any coordination can result from independent processes of growth.

The idea that all social growth leads to a "natural harmony" was a fiction of the eighteenth century which no serious person can now accept as having any real value. The nineteenth as well as the twentieth century have demonstrated with overwhelming force that uncoordinated growth, whether it takes place within a nation-state or internationally, unavoidably leads to conflict.

It is therefore absolutely essential to understand that no coordinated world society can grow out of coexistence, because there is no foundation for the belief that if two social groups A and B are left to themselves, they will grow to a state of equality and natural harmony. Social growth, as all natural growth, is an uneven process and equilibrium and coordination can only be achieved purposively, not automatically, unless one likes to leave the fate of mankind to a chance, which may be infinitesimally small.

In addition, this whole assumption is made untenable by the very fact that in the twentieth century the power-projection of one country is activated by comparison with the power of another country and by corresponding plans. There is no spontaneous social growth in our age, only guided social growth, but the guidance is upon the basis of national and bloc goals, not upon the basis of the universal goals of a world society.

The situation which is likely to result from uncoordinated growth can be projected in a very general manner.

If we have two groups A and B, we can roughly calculate the actual social power at a given moment and we can also calculate the rate of change for periods of, for instance, ten years:

Group A

1910

Rate of change: X
for each ten-year period
1910–1960

Group B

1910

Rate of change: Y
for each ten-year period
1910–1960

If Y > X, we can make an estimate of the future relationship of X and Y, even if there is a period in which the power of A and B seems to run parallel. On the other hand, the rate of social growth of A and B is obviously a variable and not a constant, while the growing social space of A and B is not only partially determined by the relation AB, but also partially by the relations AC, AD, AE, AF, etc. as well as by BC, BD, BE, BF, etc.

If one takes into account that we have not only two power-blocs, but N additional states, while composition, cohesion, etc. of the two power-blocs themselves change continuously, it is obvious that we can aim for a vision, but not for a scientific picture of world society.

Our preoccupation with scientific thinking makes us ignore the fact that we need the vision, even if we cannot achieve a scientific picture, though we should aim for this at the same time.

All social change, however, starts with a certain vision which gradually becomes more concrete and is processed by the various social groups and the various sciences until it becomes individualized in its ultimate stage.

All thinking about international society must start with the realisation that this society is at present in a state of chaos and confusion and that it hovers continuously upon the brink of disaster. Brinkmanship is no statesmanship, but rather the lack of it, at least from a global viewpoint.

In order to remedy the state of chaos and confusion, the first need lies in a vision of a coordinated society, but starting from the reality of the present. To give a recipe for harmony is simple enough; to achieve it is a tremendous task for which everybody should mobilize his forces as most nations now do for their own specific goals.

One cannot combat nationalism with more nationalism, but only by looking for a solution on different levels, either supra- or sub-national.

While the nineteenth century attributed its ills to class-conflicts and nationalism, the twentieth century shows bloc-conflicts and national conflicts. It would be tempting to regard the bloc-conflicts as externalized and nationalized class-conflicts, but this would be an oversimplification.

We may return for the moment to the observation that the nineteenth century brought us the realisation that internal tensions and external conflicts seem to influence one another. Outer aggressiveness will rarely result from inner harmony, at least not in social stages in which wars are fought by entire nations rather than by independently functioning groups.

If we apply this to the twentieth century, this means that we cannot consider international problems by themselves, but that we must relate them to the internal situation. This relationship which has not been investigated satisfactorily up to the present time is of crucial significance because all international machinery is useless if inner tensions give rise to external conflicts.

The international decision-makers are to an overwhelming extent national officials, and in this capacity they react to internal situations, quite apart from their own private motivation. Thus, a satisfactory world-condition can only be achieved if the internal situation in the largest number of countries, including the most powerful ones, is balanced. It is entirely erroneous to assume that an international equilibrium is possible if there is a lack of equilibrium within nations comprising a significant part of the world population.

This poses a serious dilemma because rapid socio-economic change is the key-motive in many countries, so that it is essential to investigate to what extent plans for national expansion may create international tensions or whether they are on the whole conducive to global equilibrium. Also in this respect, expansion must be seen in its internal as well as external facets, and its psychological implications for the national decision-makers, who may be faced with a serious dualism, must be taken into account.

This dualism of internal and external relations makes it essential to develop forms of thought in which this dualism is overcome or in which there is at least awareness of the existence of this dualism.

The fact that the individual acts in a number of social roles, as has been brought to the fore in sociological studies, is also highly significant for the study of international problems.

While nineteenth century rationalism saw Man only in one role, viz. as a rationally behaving citizen, it has become quite clear that Man as a social actor performs a number of roles which can even be rationally contradictory as long as they correspond to his life-goals. These life-goals are by no means a rational entity, socially speaking, but they form a complex structure of physical, mental and psychic needs which result in a given behavior-pattern, resulting from the inner structure and the external conditions (nature and other people). If one of these two factors changes, there can be very sudden changes in the behavior-pattern.

The coexistence of an internal and an external behaviour-pattern, speaking now from the viewpoint of a nation-state, can be analysed much more adequately by modern science (sociology, psychology, physiology and biology) than by the rational thinking of the nineteenth century that was in reality mostly wishful thinking.

The possibilities for investigating dual roles or dual behavior patterns has increased, and it is no longer adequate to repeat ad nauseam the postulate of rational behaviour, but one must investigate the roots of actual behaviour so far as modern science permits.

For these reasons the dual role of the national-international decision-maker must first be accepted as a given social fact and probed as to its causes and configuration-system.

When is it more marked? Under what conditions does it seem to diminish? These are the pertinent questions.

As the dominant international communication forms use static concepts rather than dynamic ones, there is an obvious tension between internal dynamism and external statism. This dualism between dynamism and statism puts a burden on the terminology of international communications, as in social reality internal dynamism leads in most cases sooner or later to external dynamism, or to use the conventional word: to expansionism.

It is no mark of great wisdom to assert that it is easier to change terminology than social reality, and one of the most pressing needs is to find adequate expression for the internal dynamism – external statism dualism by bringing the factor of internal change more fully within the conceptual pattern of international thinking.

Much can be gained by recognising that dynamism and statism are relative terms, and that we have to deal with the varying rates of the internal dynamism of numerous states and with a low rate of international dynamism so that there is a very serious cause of tensions which cannot be expressed at the international level.

The obvious logical conclusion is to increase international dynamism (progressive social change), and this is done via the international agencies, technical assistance and the aid programmes of various nations, but one cannot claim that the problem of national versus international dynamism is being faced in all its implications and in an exhaustive fashion, though there is general awareness that this problem must somehow be solved.

About the goals as well as about the methods there is no clarity.

What degree of dynamism do we envisage for world society?

The jurist might seek the answer in a sort of weighted and functional federalism, like that which one sees developing in W. Europe. The economist might say that the goal is a world which transforms itself gradually into a universal high-standard-of-living society.

The sociologist might attempt to visualize a world society as an entity which, if no outer pressures exist, will show a high degree of differentiation and variation rather than uniformity. He would visualize a highly complex but coordinated society in which the motivations and attitudes caused by fear would be greatly reduced.

The thought-patterns of the dominant groups, namely the Western and Communist ones are neither very explicit in their views of a coordinated world-society, nor do they indicate the methods by which the existing state of affairs could be changed in the desired direction.

It is nevertheless absolutely essential that the question how a coordinated world society can be visualized should be answered more concretely, because a certain uniformity in our thinking about the future is necessary if we are to agree about the methods. Agreement about the methods without agreement about the goals can create a dangerous situation, because methods like aid can be used for particular goals as well as for general ones.

The degree of dynamism which would be "normal" for a coordinated world society has to become related to the rate of dynamism of the individual countries of the present time. As a coordinated world society could not display overly sharp divisions of prosperity, it is obvious that a high degree of dynamism on the part of a backward country is entirely positive. In order to avoid future tensions, it is nevertheless essential to link the development rates of dynamic societies to a "normal expansion rate" of a fully developed society. If we put the rate of a dynamic country at X and that of the fully developed country at Y, there has to be a certain relationship between X and Y, because if Y were to show a cumulative increase, Y at a given moment would become larger than X, and this would mean that there would develop tensions beyond the degree commensurate to a coordinated world society.

This problem is a very crucial one, and it should be faced squarely and dealt with upon the international level from the legal, economic and sociological viewpoint. To ignore its full implications might result in our reaching a point at which socio-economic development creates international tensions rather than it reduces them, as the vague humanitarian philosophy of progress would like us to believe. This philosophy belongs to the nineteenth century rather than the twentieth which has to find matter-of-fact solutions.

CHAPTER III

THE METHOD OF THE SOCIOLOGICAL APPROACH TO INTERNATIONAL PROBLEMS

One of the originators of sociology, Auguste Comte, saw it as a great innovation that sociology, in contrast to the then prevailing systems of social philosophy, was going to approach its problems realistically and empirically by using the statistical method.

What is it that we seek te learn from the study of society? What was society like in the past, how does it look at present and what are realistic expectations for the future?

In this way one could formulate the questions which the social sciences seek to answer, and they all do this after their own fashion and with great emphasis upon their own particular perspective with which they brook no interference from other sciences.

The early stages of a "new" science are often universal, and they state certain basic facts which frequently become obscured by the great complexity of later developments.

Comte saw very clearly that all thinking about society has to be related to Man as it is Man who makes society and not vice versa. For this reason he strove hard to create an image of Man that corresponded to the basic forces of his time.

We may do likewise and ask ourselves what is the image of Man that we operate with and is it attuned to the requirements of a world society?

Not everybody will agree with this presentation of the "sociological method," but since society in general was mostly dealt with by the early sociological systems, it might be permissible for the time being to return to the "primordia rerum" of sociology.

What then is our image of Man in the twentieth century?

Although this has largely been a topic for speculative thinking, we shall attempt to follow Comte and to put the question realistically and empirically.

As one knows the tree by its fruits, one can know Man only by his actions, because these are outer manifestations that can be observed and recorded. From his actions we can draw conclusions in regard to his attributes, but even this empirical way of constructing an image of Man is hazardous and full of pitfalls so that it will be followed only in a perfunctory fashion and only so far as the content of this analysis requires.

In the study of society basic social institutions have come to the fore that are found in almost all stages and almost everywhere: an economic system; an organisational system for inner coordination and outer defense; a system of organized knowledge and belief. In other words, the farmer, or hunter, the king and the medicine-man or the priest are universal, though their functions may be combined or subdivided in different ways.

In this way, modern society does not differ from primitive societies: we still have the producers, the organisational groups and the institutions of religion, ideology and science.

If these institutions are near-universals in society, they must correspond to Man's basic attributes: the family and the economic system to physical needs and impulses; the organisational system of tribes, clans, states or regional societies to the need for defence and coordination; the religions or ideological systems to final psychic goals which place the individual in contact with Mankind as well as the universe.

As the social institutions of family, productive systems, coordinating and defense systems, and ideological or religious systems have shown great permanence as well as continuity, they will in all likelihood also be a part of the world society of the future.

The need for an economic system is self-evident and finds enough stress, if not too much. The need for an organisational system is more complex, because we think of world social organisation largely as analogous to the state, but as a world society would in all likelihood not be exposed to attacks from the outside, we need different organisational forms. The state is organized for inner coordination and outer defense while a world society will have to concern itself only with inner-coordination so that it must strive for a self-regulating, self-perpetuating and therefore decentralised system.

In order to visualize this clearly, we must attempt to overcome our predilection to think about world society as analogous to the state. World society is a totally different social form, as different from the state as the state from the family or the tribe.

This does not mean that the state will have "to wither away," but its function will have to fit into that of a self-regulating and self-perpetuating world society. States come and go; they are born and they perish. World society will have to be permanent if Man is eager to prolong his now precarious existence.

In world society there can be no brinkmanship, but only granite rockmanship. In fact, there will be fewer statesmen, because a world society will need permanence rather than change; while change needs guidance and planning, permanence needs wisdom.

For the moment, however, we should start with the realisation that the organisational forms of world society will ultimately have to become totally different from those of the nation-state. The nation-state has a centralising function; world society can only aim at decentralisation; the national society builds up the economy for defense as well as consumption; a world society will need an economy based on the consumptive needs of Mankind as a coordinated social group.

As Man has always shown a need for a ceremonial system, connected with Man's psychic problems, his aesthetic and spiritual needs and with life's basic stages: birth, puberty, marriage and death, these ceremonial systems will certainly continue and may even become much more elaborate again.

Man's fear of Man may largely disappear, but our cosmic fears are as perpetual as life itself, and they need to be surrounded by ceremony.

If we want to gain a realistic image of world society, we must base ourselves upon the individual "as he really is," rather than upon the individual in his role as a citizen of a nation-state. The roles of the individual will have to be recast, and in order to make him a member of a world society we must strengthen all his roles, except those by which he identifies himself exclusively with limited and selfish national interests. His national role must become secondary in relation to his global role.

The roles which the social actor performs in modern society are linked to the basic social institutions on the one hand and to his natural structure on the other hand. He can reconcile his social roles to his natural self if his social roles do not deviate too much from his basic structure.

The basic social institutions are: the family, the economy, the state, the culture, religious or ideological groups, and world society, while there are the many additional facets of small intimate groups, recreational groups, educational groups, aesthetic and artistic groups, cliques, etc., etc.

In this complexity of the modern role-pattern, all roles should and can be strengthened with the exception of the national roles and of those roles which stimulate hatred or contempt for other human groups, whether upon religious, ideological, racial, economic, social or other bases.

In other words, the roles must be either individualised or universalised. If they are individualised, our social roles approach more the natural pattern, and this is in a way the ideal solution.

On the other hand, in a society of probably far more than 3000 million people, we cannot individualize too much, and our social roles will continue to hold priority over our private ones for a long time to come, and this is quite acceptable as long as our private sphere remains sufficiently large. The universalisation of our roles is a theme that finds much attention in modern trends in international law, ideas of world government and world federation; the world religions and the world ideologies. They project the universal roles, however, quite differently, but as long as they seriously project their values as universal ones, these ideas have an ethical foundation and they can form the basis of discussion and elaboration.

Individualisation, on the other hand, is the favored theme of psychiatry and psychology, with firm support from modern literature.

Both universal and individual values must correspond to those of a normal, functioning human being.

The individual identifies himself with the groups which he considers essential to his life-goals or which are presented to him as such, though there has to be a realistic connection between the two. He has no "natural" interest in any group apart from its function. In other words, his identification with national groups or with other non-universal groups can be weakened if these groups transfer some of their essential functions to other groups, namely universal groups above or below the state-level.

As this contradicts completely the trend towards the expansion of the functions of governments, we have approached another major dilemma of world society. A functioning world society requires a decrease in the role of governments: the inner dynamics of most societies lead and have led to more government.

This dilemma seems almost insurmountable because, on the other hand, the extension of government has been the logical answer to the requirements of inner dynamism and outer stability. Governments have become the social agency which has to perform this tour de force, as otherwise world chaos would be immediate and irreparable.

In many cases this problem can hardly be solved, and many problems are transferred from the national to the international level. Whether an intermediary level between national government and world organisation might not be the answer is a question which deserves careful scrutiny.

The weight of government in modern society is a universal trend which has been caused by the class conflict within the national societies of the Western world and, more recently, by the striving for "status" of the new countries. Both these factors lead automatically to an extension of governmental bureaucracy as the guiding and planning social group which must prevent inner social conflict and strive for status in world society.

This increase in the role of governments has led to a decrease in inner conflicts, but it rather augments than diminishes the possibilities of international conflicts, though this is not very readily admitted by modern governments themselves.

It is, however, quite obvious. The need for a strong governmental role has resulted from the inner dynamism of a number of countries, and this dynamism causes tensions as well as excessive expectations for which modern government does not have an adequate answer. As a result the inner tensions and the excessive expectations become visible in the form of international tensions, particularly upon the ideological level of the East-West conflict, as the very essence of the ideological conflict is the degree of inner dynamism to which they form the conceptual response. On the other hand, every social group in power has a tendency to perpetuate itself, and this forms a very strong motive for the control-groups of modern industrial societies to strive for more permanent solutions. As it is not reasonable to assume that modern governments will voluntarily reduce their controls, one must look for a detour via more government in order to reach the ultimate goal of less government.

The tendency towards more government has become most noticeable though the creation of international organisations, which are, however, handicapped because the national governments do not transfer much of their control to the agencies which they create.

As a result these agencies are limited to the interests which the nation-states hold in common, and this realm is particularly small between the power-blocs of the East and the West.

For this reason the chances of more, but also effective government seem to lie more in regional than in global organisation, and one could defend the thesis that the detour of more government will have to pass via regional organisation, before effective global organisation can be reached.

In addition, there is the important factor that regional organisation is more palatable to the individual as well as to governments than global organisation which is at present vague and often chaotic. The regional group has common cultural values, a certain degree of propinquity and affinity, and regionalism is founded upon the sound economic basis of striving for greater unity with countries with which natural economic ties have often existed since centuries. One could also point to common political factors and a comparable legal system.

In addition, a number of areas show ethnic homogeneity, which can be helpful, though it should not be considered an essential factor. The strongest group-building factor consists without any doubt in having common interests, and this is much more pronounced in the case of the regional group than of world society in general, though one might wish this to be different.

Social reality, however, is the most effective basis for social organisation.

As the majority of the hundred states of which the world consists are not effective and self-sufficient economic units, there is the very strong motive for the formation of larger groups in which the modern economy can unfold itself.

Even the most powerful of present-day states are not economically self-sufficient, but much more than for them is there reason for small and medium states to form larger groups that are economically more effective. This trend is most evident in Western Europe, while other regional formations have strong political, cultural or linguistic motivations like the Arab League, the Organisation of American States, emerging federations in Africa, etc., but they also foster the extension of economic ties.

Thus, for the individual, regional federation has a rather convincing basis as it reflects his desires for economic and political stability and improvement without excessive risks. Although an intense desire for social change is imputed to the individual by dominant ideologies and philosophies, there is little acknowledgement of the fact that the individual does not desire improvement at the expense of stability and permanence.

The individual wants improvement within the framework of stability and permanence, but the ideologies of "accelerated social change" of many governments tend to stress change while they pay less attention to permanence and stability. These qualities are, however, of paramount importance for world society as well as for the individual, and in this way world society can find its roots in the individual as the ultimate measure of human well-being.

The regional group can achieve a better link with the individual than can either national or global society. The first is geared too much to the thought forms of the nineteenth century, and it overstresses the factor of coercion, while modern industrial society is basically a compromise society. Global society, on the hand, lacks reality, and the individual can find no real link with it so that it tends to operate in an inter-governmental vacuum that gives rise to indifference on the part of the individual. He would accept effective world government, but, as was pointed out above, there must be an intermediary link between world society and national societies as this link has been the most effective development in social reality.

For a sociological approach, it is the individual in which social organisation must be rooted, because otherwise we only develop formalistic superstructures that are incapable of meeting a challenge and which lead a largely symbolic existence. Society needs symbols, but if the distance between reality and superstructure becomes too large, underlying social forces become the decisive ones, with all the dangers of catastrophy and conflict.

The tensions which exist between the level of the individual and that of national thinking are largely due to an overprojection of the factor of change. National ideologies and philosophies impute to the individual desires for progress and change which are no longer realistic and which impose an excessive burden. This overprojection of the dynamic attributes of the individual is caused by the status-desires of national societies, and this problem is therefore at the same time an internal as well as an external one.

The individual wants change and progress, but not at the rate which control groups of national societies impute to him. The stronger the power drive of a national society, the heavier the burdens which are placed upon the individual, while, and this cannot be repeated often enough, a world society requires that only moderate and normal burdens are placed upon the individual.

Modern society still has to find the equation between the efforts it requires from the individual and the rewards which it offers to him. In the societies of the Western world the rewards are high in material goods, but the efforts are often one-sided, monotonous and cause emotional frustration, particularly because there is no feeling of solidarity and permanence. In the dynamic societies, on the other hand, the striving for national power status has priority over individual goals, though the idea of a world society could make the achievement of higher socio-economic status a goal which can be reached gradually. It is again the feeling of emotional uncertainty and fear which makes it possible for status-projections completely to dominate individual goals, though the latter are presented as part of the former.

The greatest problem lies in determining what regional groups in world society form "natural social groups" on which the future can be built and in which the individual can find normal emotional satisfaction.

To expect this from an egalitarian, high-powered world society is unrealistic as this society is nowhere on the horizon, and the high-powered superstates of the present only maintain themselves with the aid of a constantly presented image of impending attack. This is hardly a normal situation and no normal society will develop under a continuous threat, real or imagined, of disaster.

As "natural regions" of the world one could designate: the United States and Canada, Western Europe, the Commonwealth countries, the Soviet Union with Eastern Europe, China and adjoining territories, the Arab League, India and adjoining countries, Latin America, Central America, emerging federations in Africa.

Most of these regions have shown a long and gradual development; they have common forms of thought, common ambitions, and they have the enormous advantage of propinquity or a developed communications system. They are "real" to the individual.

They also run parallel to the power blocs, but they would mean a certain decentralisation of the power blocs. This trend, which is clearly visible in the relations between the United States and W. Europe and between the Soviet Union and China can only benefit world society. A greater independence of Eastern Europe and a modus vivendi between Western and Eastern Europe would also go a long way towards a functioning world society, without requiring any sudden change in the power structure.

The form of organisation these regions would require is entirely their own concern. The Europe of the Six strives for a formal structure; the Europe of the Seven does not. The Arab League shows unity towards the non-Arab world, while internally it shows variety and differentiation. The most important and difficult matter is to visualize China as a strong regional society, but this would be highly preferable to the present trend towards a world divided into two power blocs which compete for world domination.

Nevertheless, the power blocs are the dominant social groups of the present time, but it might be possible to place other social forms alongside them so that they acquire a stronger infrastructure, while this might make more cross-bloc contacts possible. If the blocs feel sure of their power in regard to certain regions, there might be less competition in regard to the developing areas, and the latter might find their own solutions with the aid of international and regional organisations. The regional organisation might be a means of preventing the fragmentation of aid and the giving of aid for political purposes. Much of this is already done by the United Nations and the affiliated agencies, but there is still considerable room for the extension of regional organisation. While it seems almost impossible to coordinate the planning of a hundred different states, interregional coordination would be much more feasible.

The regional organisation has obviously a preference for propinquity, but, sociologically speaking, a region is any multi-state group which has a developed communications system and a certain amount of political and economic coordination. It often shows more unity seen from the outside than it does from the inside. This is, for instance, the case with the Commonwealth countries, as well with the West or the Communist countries.

International legal principles like national sovereignty, self-determination and non-interference in the affairs of other states give a certain amount of independence to states which belong to blocs, but national independence has largely become a relative concept. It can be used by states to build up a whole network of international relations, while politically they may continue to belong to a bloc.

To make the world more normal, the relative freedom of the state is a useful principle because it will enable states to develop the most advantageous relationships, and these will often be regional ones. Power blocs lead to economic distorsions and extensive centralisation: a normal world society will need a natural economy, based upon practical rather than power considerations.

The power mentality remains the greatest danger to our world, and it is extremely difficult to state exactly in what forms this power mentality shows itself. It hides behind political concepts, as in the case of power-communism, but it is also present in the high standard of living philosophy which creates useless needs and keeps the individual chained to the wheels of an overly complex economy.

To create a normal world, we must begin by developing a normal mentality and this is not only the task but also the interest of the individual, who suffers perhaps more from having a power-mentality than from being subjected to it. A power mentality is often a reaction to having been subjected to the expansionism of others in the past. Present power desires are often the result of having been on the receiving end of power in the past, and in cases like this, it is reasonable to expect that the power mentality will need some time and some room for expansion to work itself off. The absence of resistance to it is as bad as too much resistance to it, which makes the power desire explosive. It can only be restrained by the image of a normal world in which nations and groups of nations have their natural place.

This is an extremely difficult and delicate problem that can best be approached by taking the dynamic potential of a social group as a real social force that cannot be ignored or suppressed, but only channelled into constructive directions.

The rate of social change of nations can be roughly calculated but it is much more difficult to make the results of these estimates motives for international action.

All nations have the right to grow and develop, but the processes of growth must be coordinated and controlled if we are to avoid chaos. This is in general widely admitted, but little is done to give concrete form to this vague philosophy. And concreteness in this respect is synonymous with coordination and order.

CHAPTER IV

INTERNATIONAL LAW AND SOCIOLOGY

International law is and has been the strongest force for the ordering of international society. This is not surprising as law is the dominant means of social control of governments, and international society is largely shaped by the policies of national governments and of international agencies which have been constructed analogously to national governments.

If international law were not only the preferred means of intergovernmental communications, but also the dominant motive of international action, there would no longer be any international problems of alarming propensities, and there would already be an ordered world society, as we actually have in many respects during normal periods in which no major violent conflicts occur.

There is, however, a conflict between the principles of international law as motives for international action and international law as a means of communication that can be adjusted to specific political purposes. Analysis of this conflict no longer raises a legal problem, but a sociological one or one with which the sciences of politics, international relations and social psychology deal.

In German philosophy great attention has always been given to the problem of the "Is" and the "Ought," but the question why some people do not always behave as some other people would like them to was never quite resolved. In the same way, we have the problem of why some nations, mostly large ones, do not behave as other nations, mostly small or medium ones, would wish them to.

There is undoubtedly no right to power, and no legal system can uphold such right. On the other hand, the outlawing of power would not show any results if there is such a thing as an innate power drive. The power drive ignores law in the moral sense, though it may still use it in its function as a means of communications, or as a means of regulating the use of armed force.

Within ordered national societies, law protects all citizens, because governments show sufficient self-discipline, and perhaps because they are aware that the continuity of their control depends upon an impersonal social order. In the same way, the efficacy of international law depends upon the feeling of responsibility for world order of the major states.

In this way, law is first and foremost a moral responsibility as it has been seen by great jurists like Suarez, Vitoria, Hugo Grotius and others.

The positivist school of international law has attempted to separate law completely from morality, but this trend is again losing ground in a period in which new states are striving to orient themselves in international society.

The positivist interpretation was the dominant one when a small number of states held the upper hand and when there was a strong interest in using international law as a means of preserving the status quo. In that period the idea of the equality of states and of national sovereignty was acceptable, because the leading states were not too unequal, while there were in addition common civilisational principles.

To see the state as a static and abstract social group has been one of the major tenets of international law, as it did not develop a conceptual scheme which was also capable of dealing with changes in the power structure. The tendency to maintain international law in its forms of the nineteenth century has made it lose a great deal of its moral prestige, though its role as a means of intergovernmental communication has vastly increased, due to the extension of international contacts and to the increase in the number of states.

International law has developed analogously to the national legal system of the Western countries of the New Era, and this influence has given it some of its major characteristics.

The political ideas of liberty, equality and brotherhood of the eighteenth century dominated not only the internal legal development of the Western countries, but they found their exact counterpart in international law in the concepts of self-determination, the equality of states and the "family of nations."

These ideas were obviously postulated in the period in which they were created, as none of the qualities mentioned existed in social reality. When they were given the legal form of the contractual freedom of the individual, of political and moral equality, they acted within a society that had still many structural characteristics in terms of privileged groups. Within the states of the West, the contractual equality of the citizens did not lead to any real social equality. It benefited mostly the middle classes while the workers had to organize themselves as groups before they achieved better socio-economic status.

Political equality also became a technique used by organised groups rather than individuals, and the result of this political equality has become quite different from what its originators visualised.

It has become quite evident that the individualistic concepts of the New Era had to be compensated by collectivist trends and movements, before an equilibrated society resulted. It must also be pointed out that this greater social harmony was only achieved through the extension of governmental functions and of a governmental bureaucracy. As a general conclusion, it could be stated that the principles of the freedom and equality of the individual worked well enough, as soon as there was sufficient control over the egotism of individuals and groups.

In international society, there is no comparable situation. The principle of the equality of states has much less reality than the principle of the equality of citizens. An individual may be rich or poor, strong or weak, intelligent, or stupid, but he is still *one* person and subject to the laws of a stronger group, namely government.

States can consist of hundreds of millions of citizens, or of a few thousand; they can control a tremendous territory or a very small one; they can have staggering industrial power or practically none at all.

The equality of states has become in some respects an unrealistic principle in the twentieth century.

Within the national states it was believed that legal equality would create social equality. This has proved a fallacy, and there is no indication that the legal equality of states is creating greater international equality. On the contrary, the distance between strong and weak states is far greater at present than in the nineteenth century, while blocs of states have become more important than single ones.

It is also frequently asserted that the fictitious equality of states creates a moral responsibility on the part of larger states to treat the small ones as equals. This functions quite well under normal conditions, but it has less reality as soon as an emergency arises, as the two world wars demonstrated quite convincingly.

The right of self-determination is no more than a legalisation of chaos. If a hundred states can follow their own volition there can be no question of order. The idea of self-determination contradicts that of a legal order: there can be either the one or the other.

This reconfirms the fact that international law functions best as a set of moral principles: to constitute a positivist legal order it requires a centralised control system such as the nation-states possess. Its coercive power is largely a moral factor, and as such it is highly important.

In the philosophy of international law we can still find the social thinking of the eighteenth century in terms of the principle that the freedom of the individual leads to social harmony because the individual will "by nature" have consideration for the right of others. This same assumption still prevails in our international thinking when we assume that the independence and legal equality of states will result in harmony.

As this assumption proved erroneous in regard to the internal development of the Western countries where excessive individualism led to the class struggle, it would be wiser to revise our thinking about international society if we do not want the recurrence of the class struggle on an international scale and in staggering dimensions.

There is much awareness of this problem, and this has given rise to the idea that we must achieve a better distribution of global income in order to forestall conflict. The Technical Assistance Programmes of the United Nations, UNICEF, FAO, etc. are all operating upon the basis of this assumption, and so are the large and some of the smaller nations in terms of individual aid programmes.

Although much is achieved, the structure of world society is affected only very moderately by these efforts, and only very gradually is there a shift to a more equitable distribution.

It seems obvious that a certain socio-economic equalisation can be achieved much better by regions than by individual states, unless they are large ones and, in the latter case, the power motive becomes immediately mixed with the motive of economic amelioration.

The increase in the number of the states which all strive for status makes the problem more difficult instead of simpler. In addition, there is the fact that violent conflict between states has frequently occurred because state A wants to prevent state B from dominating the weaker region C. The motivation has often been that B + C would be more powerful than A, and therefore A goes to war to prevent this development.

In order to forestall such developments, all aid-giving would have to be rigidly controlled, and should take place only via international or regional agencies. In addition, it has to be borne in mind that aid will only be effective if a country itself shows sufficient dynamism; otherwise it might do more harm than good.

As dynamic development is the key motive of present-day world society, we can only expect an ordered world society if these dynamic forces can be brought within the context of law and social control.

This would only seem possible if a more realistic relationship could be achieved between actual socio-economic power and legal representation, including changes in this representation commensurate to actual power changes.

One sees the beginnings of this in the regional organisations where the principle of weighted representation has become the accepted one. Relatively greater weight is given to small countries, but there is nevertheless a relationship between the "weight" of a socio-economic group and the number of votes of which it disposes.

In world society this problem is far more complicated because there are not only the existing "weight differences," but also the differing rates of social development which would have to find legal expression. It would not be satisfactory to use the standard-of-living as a standard because this would put a premium on consumption and industrialisation, and countries should have the liberty to evolve the social system they desire, particularly if we visualize an ordered world society.

Nevertheless, it should not be impossible to devise formulas by which the countries receive legal representation in relation to their "weight," although representation proportional to population is neither desirable, nor possible. Since the problem has been tentatively solved regionally, it can be either expanded to other regions or considered upon a world-wide scale.

The major difficulty is that the factor of change has not yet been visualised clearly. What happens if the population of a country decreases or if its socio-economic status diminishes? Obviously its "weight" would have to be reduced, but there will be such emotional resistance that it would be better to visualize upward, than downward movement and to devise a formula by which the "weight" of a given country could be increased.

In spite of the complexity and difficulty of this problem, it should be faced squarely if we want to reduce international tensions.

If country A were to succeed in building up its socio-economic status, and if its international weight were increased accordingly, there would be much less frustration. Obviously, such a development would only be feasible if all factors like climate, value-system, etc. were taken into consideration, and if small countries were given proportionately a greater weight than large ones, in order to retain the moral aspect of the principle of legal equality.

A country which gives its citizens an adequate life should be considered as fully qualified. There should be no preference given to a high standard of living over a normal one, as the high standard of living philosophy is often too much related to power desires and expansion.

As a natural division of labor can be better achieved regionally than by individual states, it is again the development of the region, with a legal system based on proportional representation, which comes to the fore, though new regions may have a preference for equal representation as long as the region has not acquired more stable social forms.

It is also in the region that a certain correspondence develops between regional and national law while this is much less true of the relationship between international and national law, though there are encouraging developments.

As all law consists of rules made by individuals for other individuals, there must be a certain parallelism between national, regional and international law if we are to achieve a functioning world order. At present the systems are often contradictory, particularly in regard to the factor of social change which receives full or even excessive weight in national or regional law, but almost no acknowledgement upon the global level, at least in a concrete form. If people change, states change, and this cannot be argued away legally.

The state is no more than a social group organised in terms of a territorial unit, and as such it should find legal expression, shorn of all its fictitious attributes which it acquired as a class group rather than as a territorial group in the course of the New Era. The majority of the people of a given country do not believe in the equality of states, or in their self-determination, or in their power, dignity, or superiority. These are all the fictions of the ruling classes of bygone periods. No service is rendered to the world by creating such classes in new countries: on the contrary, they need simple, effective and efficient leadership.

Under national law, a group of ten people does not receive the same weight as a single individual. Why then change this completely normal principle when dealing with territorial groups in terms of states. One hundred million people is more than two million people and every human being is aware of this.

The criteria should be size, population and adequate development. Under-development would mean reduced legal weight, while it would not be very practical to suggest reductions for over-development, though this might be morally desirable as over-development easily creates international tensions.

The moralist, however, has no chance of becoming the international decision-maker, but the realist might.

It seems at any rate a justified conclusion that one of the most pressing problems is the reconsideration of the position of the state in international law, and a more realistic evaluation of the state, not as an abstract entity, but as a given social group which functions as a territorial unit.

This group must receive a legal weight which stands in a realistic relationship to social reality, though this does not mean one in direct proportion to its numbers.

Taking the existing position as a starting point, the following possibilities seem reasonable:

1) A legal distinction between large, medium and small states, and a corresponding "weight" formula.

2) A formula by which the weight is adjusted in accordance with socio-economic power, in ratio to population, territory, resources and value-system.

A country which considers its socio-economic conditions as corresponding to its value-system should not be forced into development in order to gain higher international status. It will receive full status if it declares its socio-economic condition to be satisfactory, thereby abandoning its claim to international aid.

This may sound old-fashioned, but it is the system which prevailed within many countries until recently. World society cannot jump to the status of a fully developed society, but can only reach this by stages, and these stages can be visualized by a comparison with the development within national states. Within the state, democratic rights were first linked to certain qualifications, and only gradually was there an expansion linked with the extension of education and the achieving of a higher socio-economic status.

The sociology of international law concentrates on the relationship between law and the social system, and this relationship is more complex than was assumed in the past. Every given social situation is based upon a structural relationship between unequal factors. In fact, their relative inequality is the condition of the relationship because complete equality in every respect would make any social system superfluous.

If social reality consists of a structural relationship between unequal factors, the question arises what the function of law is in regard to this structured social group. One can visualize that law expresses the existing structure of a society or that it attempts to bring about a change in this structure by giving equal status to non-equal social parties.

In the first case, one can speak of "structural law," in the second of egalitarian or equalitarian law.

Structural law is, for instance, the distinction between minors and grown-ups, between male and female, between legally responsible and non-responsible. Also the guild-law of the Middle Ages was a structural law as well as certain forms of modern labour law, like compulsory arbitration, where existing social relationships are considered in a different setting from that between equal contractual partners.

Contract law is the typical example of egalitarian law.

International law is largely contractual law in terms of contracts between legally equal partners, while regional law is an example of structural law where actually existing social relationships are taken into consideration.

Under egalitarian law country A = country B; under structural law the rights and duties of A and B differ relatively according to their actual status or at least approximately according to this actual status.

The contractual relationship in municipal law is a special legal relationship within the context of a fully developed national legal system. This system creates conditions under which the fiction of the equality of contractual partners is a pragmatic simplification.

Transference of this contractual relationship to international society is much less effective because there is no fully developed legal system within which the contractual relationship takes place.

Egalitarian law is a useful fiction in municipal law because it is dynamic and because it simplifies hundreds of complex relationships. In this way it has been seen as a dynamic tool which facilitates economic relationship and thus helps to bring about greater economic well-being and perhaps even equality.

International society is far more structured, though by natural force rather than by purposive human action, than national societies. The power difference between countries A and B is r-times greater than the power difference of citizens X and Y of countries A and B, though any direct comparison is difficult because the exercise of power within national states is restricted by the national social system, while they are only legal-moral restrictions in international society. This latter aspect also means that the release of social tensions via violence is more frequent and much more disastrous than the comparatively small use of violence within national societies.

If the power distance between social actors is great and if the recognized realm of social action is extensive, the question arises whether an egalitarian legal system or a structural one is the preferred instrument of legal control.

There must be a working relationship between law and social reality. If the legal rules are too much at variance with reality, they will be ignored. If they attempt to adjust to reality too closely, they would prevent motion and change.

In regard to international society, the distance between law and social reality has increased since the nineteenth century, and this would argue in favor of an increase in structural law, i.e. a closer relationship between international reality and international law.

Thus, adopting a different approach we arrive again at the conclusion that the most pressing need is to change the legal expression of the state from that of an abstract and static entity to that of a living and dynamic social group, which has attributes not unlike those of the individual because we deal with a group composed of individuals and having reality only as a factor in the mentality of individuals.

As the individual who functions as an international decision-maker is in almost all cases a functionary of a nation-state, we would only render him a service by making his task more concrete. He does not actually represent the abstract entity country A, but he represents so many people: the citizens of country A and, more specifically, the control group of country A.

The possibility of expressing the frustrations of country A or of its control group is only increased by the use of the semi-mystical language which we apply when speaking about states. If we see the international decision-makers as having a mandate from X people, making up country A, matters become more realistic, while we also express the fact that the policy-maker has only a mandate from his own fellow-citizens and not for mankind as a whole. If the policy-maker were to represent a number of people roughly comparable to that of other representatives, international meetings would gain a far more realistic aspect.

Now A, representing 200 million people, is followed by B, representing 2 million people, and both speak in vague, mystical terms about the missionary tasks of their respective countries.

It is no wonder that mankind is losing faith in international assemblies: this is not the fault of mankind, but rather of the assemblies.

CHAPTER V

THE SOCIOLOGICAL JURISTS

It was perhaps, to a large extent, due to the dominance of rationalism that a rather wide divergence developed between law and social reality. The basic assumption of rationalism, viz. of human reason as the basis of society, made it tempting for the jurist to erect rational structures which were deemed to be in correspondence with the actual forms of society as a rational institution.

Neither the philosophers of the Middle Ages, nor the adherents of natural law would have admitted this assumption while the nineteenth and twentieth century saw the rise of collectivist movements for which a rational society was still an ultimate goal, but an intervening period of dynamic social movement was visualised in which centralized control was to take precedence over the liberty of the supposedly rational individual.

Socialism, particularly in its Marxist form, adhered to the rationalist theory of progress, but this progress was to be a scientifically controlled process rather than one that depended upon the volition of independent individuals.

The struggle between individualism and collectivism was not a struggle between rationalism and irrationalism, but a conflict between rationalism as interpreted by a majority of individuals and a dynamic rationalism, guided by a scientific elite.

The rationalism of the eighteenth century had become too static for the subsequent period of the industrial revolution, and a dynamic rationalism leads to different social precepts rather than a static rationalism.

For a static rationalism the individual is already rational; for a dynamic rationalism he has to be made rational by a scientifically constructed society of which the elite holds the formula for rational social development.

The latter view introduces a dynamic element which was absent in the former one.

As the former one had dominated legal development, it is obvious that a divergence grew between rational individualist law and rational socialist law aimed at a future society.

While this divergence has led to the creation of a Western legal system and a socialist legal system, there has been collectivist influence in Western thought, while in socialist law there has been a certain continuity in relation to the private and the commercial sphere.

In the Western world, it was increasingly felt that law as a logical-rational structure might at times be at variance with actual social conditions, so that a number of corrections were made, not only in practice, but also in theoretical thinking.

Rationalism had assumed that a logically consistent legal structure would bring about the desired rational society, by using coercion in the cases in which the natural impulse of reason was not sufficiently developed. In other words, law was seen as an instrument of social amelioration, but the actual developments of industrial society did not sustain this view. In fact, the growing class conflict made it quite obvious that law only functions if a certain social equilibrium is already given. If there is no equilibrium, law alone cannot create a balanced society, but amelioration must first set in in the socio-economic sphere.

Consequently there are two possibilities: law can carry out its function if a sense of social solidarity does already prevail or, in the absence of an equilibrium, solidarity must first be established in the socio-economic or cultural sphere before law can gain the desired degree of normal efficacy. The efficacy of law does not depend in the first place upon the inner consistency of the legal system which can develop rationally while society does not, but it depends upon a functioning social structure. In this view, law is not by itself capable of ameliorating society, but it needs a solidaristic society in order to function.

If law and society do not show a direct parallelism, but stand in a relationship of interaction, it becomes essential for the jurist to concern himself with the actual conditions of a society, in order to be able to develop a constructive legal philosophy which is pragmatic rather than rational.

The adherents of this latter view one might term the sociological jurists, while those who believe that the inner consistency of the legal system is their foremost concern are the traditional jurists. As in most trends of legal thinking, this divergence showed itself in municipal legal thinking before it also gained influence in regard to international law.

There is no reason here to go into the controversy between law as the expression of class interests and law as the expression of popular will. In all actual legal systems, both elements are present as the law-maker himself belongs to the social control group, but he has to take into consideration the interests of society as a whole. A certain preference may exist in his mentality favoring the employer rather than the worker, the industrial class over the agricultural, etc. but in a stable society those possibilities have their natural limits. While a dynamic society might operate in terms of postulates and priorities, it cannot force change too far beyond the actual capabilities and normal volition of the citizens if it is concerned about its own social continuity. The conflict between Western and Communist views of law has become so distorted by political tensions that these views cannot be brought constructively within the framework of a theoretical comparison.

It must suffice for the purpose of this investigation to point to the two types of theory: the one which sees law as an independent social system that derives its function from its inner rationality and the other which sees law as rooted in social customs and social solidarity and as deriving its strength from those roots. As a third view, one could mention the idea that law as a part of the social superstructure must be buttressed by civilisational, religious, ideological or ethical principles in order to gain the desired degree of efficacy. This latter view, however, concentrates its attention upon the necessary attributes of the social superstructure, while the sociological school is mostly concerned about the interaction between social reality and the social superstructure, without going too much into the subdivisions of the superstructure itself, like law, religion, ideology, ethics, culture-values, etc.

For the adherents of the sociological approach, actual social reality and the flow of social life, perhaps partially submerged in the subconscious, are at the root of our society, while the superstructure as the conscious creation of values is always somewhat limited by being a rationalisation post hoc. All that we are socially conscious of belongs for a considerable part to the past, and we must seek to adjust ourselves to the underlying forces of society if we are to strive for permanence and stability. This means that we must try to foresee natural developments rather than attempt to perpetuate existing conditions or to shape reality according to a preconceived pattern.

It is this link with reality which has been stressed in the sociological schools of legal thinking, though it should be pointed out that this change in outlook was more marked on the European continent than in the Anglo-Saxon countries. The common law system is more elastic and more pragmatic than the civil law which went to the extreme of assuming all possibilities of social action, even in regard to the future.

The conflict between individualist and collectivist trends of thinking reached its peak on the European continent, partly because it was there, particularly in France, that rationalism achieved its fullest flowering. In addition there was the tremendous impact of the thinking of the exact sciences which resulted in the idea that a complete social control system was quite possible in a rational society. This proved fallacious because not sufficient room was given to the social dynamism of the emerging industrial societies.

As rationalist legal thinking had been most pronounced on the Continent, it is also there that we find the first re-emergence of efforts to point to a link between law and social reality. This trend dominated the historical school of German legal thinking as well as the solidarism of Duguit, who saw law as the expression of social solidarity rather than as its creator.

In the domain of international law it was the Swiss jurist Max Huber who first advocated strongly that international law must also be seen in relation to its social foundations. In his essay "Beiträge zur Kenntnis der soziologischen Grundlagen des Völkerrechts und der Staatengesellschaft,"[1] Huber pointed out that the state has become so instrumental in shaping our thought-patterns that it is difficult to think about world society in terms which are sufficiently realistic.

The dominance of the state has caused a certain neglect of the study of international relations, because only the segment which has bearing on the activity of state organs was deemed worthy of theoretical investigation.[2]

Max Huber draws attention to the fact that the rules of a social group develop first with a relative closeness to reality, but they tend to show a life of their own as they become institutionalized. This process of increasing independence is due to the growth of social complexity which makes

[1] In: *Jahrbuch des öffentlichen Rechts der Gegenwart,* IV, 1960, pp. 56–134. Also in his "Die soziologischen Grundlagen des Völkerrechts. Mit einer Vorbemerkung von Hubert Kraus," Berlin, Grünewald (Rothschild), 1928. *Internationalrechtliche Abhandlungen.*

[2] B. Landheer, "Contemporary sociological theories and international law." In: *Académie de Droit International, Recueil des Cours,* 1957, I. Vol. 91. pp. 27–43.

it impossible to formulate general rules in any simple form, while the professionalization of law creates specific forms in regard to its application and interpretation. This process of institutionalization of law increases the distance between law and social reality, though there obviously always remains a certain amount of interaction.

In international law, according to Huber, the distance between law and social reality is less than in national law, because the state is creator as well as subject of the law. This also makes it evident that international law can only be effective in so far as there are collective interests among states. In this way, Huber also explains the principle of the equality of states as expressing the intention of the most powerful states not to extend their dominance over weaker countries. In other words, it is the legal expression of a certain equilibrium, but as soon as the equilibrium becomes disturbed, the principle also loses its efficacy.

To Max Huber the existence of a certain equilibrium was a prerequisite for the functioning of international law. It expressed an equilibrium rather than created one. If one used the formula international law = common interests of the most powerful states, then it is obvious that this realm is narrower at present than in the nineteenth century, though it would be enough for an equilibrium if the avoidance of war would become the dominant motive of the most powerful states.

So far as our present period is concerned, it is useful to remember that Max Huber considered a decrease in the role of state governments as the conditio sine qua non for a functioning world society. He put more faith in the development of self-controlling social groups below the state level than in a world government superimposed upon national governments, as this would only be feasible if national governments voluntarily reduced their role. And of this there has been little evidence. Huber was particularly concerned about the mass suggestion that national states exercise upon their populations and which is not conducive to the emergence of a balanced world society.

Since the period in which Max Huber wrote about the sociological foundations of international law, we have witnessed the emergence of powerful ideological groups, while the great increase in the number of states has given world society a far more complex structure of which the attributes are not as yet clearly visible.

A different sociological approach was used by Georg Schwarzenberger in his article "Jus pacis ac belli. Prolegomena to a sociology of international law."[3] His analysis is based upon the fundamental sociological distinction between society and community, originally made by the German sociologist Toennies.

Law can only develop its typical function of providing rational rules for conduct in so far as a society has transformed itself into a community and is no longer frustrated by the overriding power of "over-mighty subjects." A second condition is that there is an organized coercive power in order to enforce legal rules against recalcitrant members.

International law, according to Schwarzenberger, does not condition, but is conditioned by the rule of force. International law expresses power relationships instead of regulating them. Consequently, it expresses the volition of dominant states and changes in accordance with the power structure of world society.

As an example of this, one can mention such rules as title by conquest for the acquisition of territory or the exclusion of duress as a ground for invalidating a peace treaty. The rules on, for instance, diplomatic immunity and administrative rules are in different categories, because the first are based upon reciprocity and represent a beginning of integration while the administrative rules, for instance on air navigation, are a clear reflection of already existing common interests.

International law consists of power law, law based upon reciprocity or rational law and law of coordination. Only the two latter categories are law in the proper meaning of the term and while they show a strong quantitative development, the segment of power law has not diminished if one were to measure it in terms of the military expenditures of the majority of states, which constitute a far higher percentage of national income than in the nineteenth century.

If international law is interpreted as a law of power, reciprocity and coordination, it can be classified accordingly as an ideology, reality and utopia.

These elements are present in any legal system, but in relation to international society the power element is the dominant one and it has been increasing rather than diminishing, perhaps because the emerging structure of world society is neither clearly visible nor acknowledged in

[3] In: *The American Journal of International Law,* XXXVII, n. 3, 1943, pp. 460–479. Cf. also his "International law and society," in *The Yearbook of world affairs,* I, 1947, pp. 159–177, and "The interdisciplinary treatment of international law," in *Grundprobleme des internationalen Rechts,* Festschrift für Jean Spiropoulos, Bonn, 1957, pp. 401–411.

our thinking, so that a general condition of fear and uncertainty prevails. In order to reduce these tensions, there are many international activities which must be seen as compensation-mechanisms rather than as being functional. They fall into the category which Schwarzenberger describes as "utopian."

While Schwarzenberger has examined international law in relation to power, F.S.C. Northrop [4] concentrated on the aspect of the efficacy of international law. Basing his theory upon the sociology of law of Ehrlich, Northrop distinguishes between living law and positive law. The habitual and traditional behavior-patterns of social groups form the living law, while the positive legal system is the representation of these patterns in legal form.

Northrop is of the opinion that the living law of the various civilisations does not differ as much as the positivist legal systems which often represent more the living law of the past than that of the present. In this way, the living law of the various civilizations could be made the basis of a new system of international law.[5]

Northrop sees the behaviour-patterns of social groups as the response to the challenge of the natural and social environment.

Although this idea is appealing and can be used effectively to analyze behaviour-patterns, it acknowledges existing differences rather than offers a possibility of diminishing them. If group A has grown to great power, partly as a result of its own vitality, partly as a result of having met effectively the challenges of the natural and social environment, power is acknowledged as a natural fact, and this type of explanation does not make clear why group A should voluntarily reduce its own power in favor of group B, unless the growing power of B constitutes a new challenge, to which A adjusts itself by becoming more "peaceful." This could reduce the challenge of A to B, but if the growing process of B has already gained sufficient momentum, the compromise between A and B might no longer be possible. In fact, the power of A, which might be in a process of consolidation, and the growing power of B only go through a relatively brief period in which the establishment of an equilibrium becomes possible.

An equilibrium does not presuppose power equality, which does not

[4] See F. S. C. Northrop, *Naturalistic and cultural foundations for a more effective international law,* Yale Law Journal, LIX, No. 8, 1950, pp. 1430–1450.
[5] *Ibid.*

really exist in nature, but only such a relationship between A and B that the weight of A is sufficient to check the process of B's growth up to a point lying somewhat below the power of A. As soon as the power of B outgrows that of A, the greater momentum of growth of B, which acquired power later, is likely to make an equilibrium no longer possible. In history, there are numerous examples of this situation though the rapidly growing power of B may also lead to overexertion and overestimation so that it results in a breakdown.

In general, it seems that the conservative forces in our society outweigh the revolutionary ones, at least if history is viewed over long periods. In this way, one could support Northrop's contention of the similarity of the living law of the dominant civilisations, but only if they are viewed over a very long period. Western civilisation, Moslem civilisation, the civilisations of India and China, all have shown great continuity though their interrelationship has undergone change. It is only Russia which is the relative newcomer and which shows the momentum of growth that makes the emergence of an equilibrium precarious, though not impossible. As it is the peacemaker for a number of other countries, it is itself threatened by the momentum of their growth, more particularly by that of China, and this development might gradually make it a more conservative force.

In this way, an equilibrium becomes more possible, though it would not easily become sufficiently strong to withstand a war. This equilibrium could only grow gradually if there were no major upheavals in world society, and if there were a growing realisation that the living law of the dominant civilisations is similar, in so far as it represents the living law of industrial mass societies, which are neither capitalist nor communist in the nineteenth century meaning of the word.[6]

If seen this way, Northrop's distinction between living law and positive law is instructive, though one should also add that ideologies and official value-patterns of societies are often at variance with their living values.

In a different way, the relationship between social reality and international law is dealt with by Charles de Visscher in his "Cours général de principes de droit international public" at The Hague Academy of International Law and in his "Théories et réalités en droit international public." Charles de Visscher attributes the weakness of international law in the first place to the insecurity which prevails among the states, because at all times they can resort to war if they consider this to be in

[6] Cf. P. Sorokin.

their national interest. According to De Visscher, some progress lies in the fact that the idea of natural solidarity is no longer adhered to and that we are aware that moral values must be established purposively and consciously. They cannot be left to a vague belief in "natural harmony." The establishment of security is a psychological and a moral problem rather than a legal one, while the point of departure can be sought only in the existing condition of national egotism as the dominant motive of states.

"Nous avons certes assez de pactes et de chartes. Il ne faut en attendre rien d'effectif ou de durable sans le développment de l'esprit communautaire, sans une prise de conscience nouvelle chez les hommes des disciplines inéluctables de la sécurité collective. On a dit avec infiniment de raison "Que les guerres prenant naissance dans l'esprit des hommes, c'est dans l'esprit des hommes que doivent être élevées les défenses de la Paix" (Préambule de la Convention constitutive de l'U.N.E.S.C.O., 1945). Les procédures les plus ingénieuses, les mécanismes logiques les mieux conçus resteront lettre morte tant que le progrès moral ne nous aura pas fait franchir le seuil qui, aujourd'hui, sépare la Cité de l'Humanité. Le problème se ramène à la conception que les hommes se feront du pouvoir, au choix qu'ils feront entre un idéal de puissance nationale et un idéal de coopération internationale." [7]

In regard to the problems of global and regional security, De Visscher tends to the global viewpoint and is of the opinion that regional alliances are predominantly political and do not contribute to an atmosphere of peace. While this might be true of regional parts aimed at power, it is less relevant to regional treaties aimed at economic integration and cooperation, as long as they are conducted with a view to the economic well-being of the world in general.

In regard to international law, De Visscher is of the opinion that its study should remain rigidly juridical, but that the international jurist should also occupy himself with the science of international relations in order to acquire a more realistic view of the power structure of international society, and, in particular, of the changes in this structure which are positive and constructive and which would lead to a more functional role on the part of national governments. There is an element of choice in our social actions, and we can become aware of the demands of a coordinated world society in relation to our national policies.

[7] See page 546. Ch. de Visscher, "Cours général de principes de droit international public," *Recueil des Cours, Académie de droit international.* 1954 II.

In this way, regional pacts can be, but are not automatically, a contribution to the building of an infrastructure between national and global forms of organisation. This might become more essential as the number of states increases. On the other hand, it should be realised that within the new states of Asia and Africa new social forms may develop below the national level which are not necessarily the same as those within the dominant countries. The process of growth towards greater coordination must take place within the states in order to make it a valid postulate between the states.

The idea that we must strive for a less simplist view of social evolution and of social progress is a point that is strongly stressed by Alejandro Alvarez in his "Le droit international nouveau dans ses rapports avec la vie actuelle des peuples." [8] The idea of social evolution and social progress has largely become a tool of propagandist forces while we need a sound, scientific and realistic analysis of social evolution in order to arrive at a responsible image of the future of world society. Business interests and ideologies in particular overstress the idea of expanding needs and a constantly expanding economy, while a coordinated and permanent world society obviously needs a rather stable economy. This simple truth is constantly obscured by economic and political power groups, which are among the main instigators of international unrest and of excessive expectations within some of the dominant countries.

One can only agree with Alvarez that it is essential that we should view the evolution towards a world society as realistically as possible. The facets of "change" must be a part of international thinking, not as a vague heuristic idea but as a rigid scientific concept that can be used to evaluate what rate of social change is conducive to the emergence of a coordinated world society.

A high rate of social change by only certain countries can be a negative rather than a positive development from the viewpoint of world society, and it is one of the key tasks of modern social science to determine the rate and type of change by each individual country or region that would be the most conducive to the emergence of a world society. While we are convinced that too little progress is damaging, we are less aware that too much individual progress by one country can have an even more negative effect by creating excessive international tensions.

Alvarez advocates the development of three new sciences, which are

[8] Paris, Editions Pédone, 1959.

necessary for the understanding of international society:

1) A science of social evolution, especially from an international viewpoint. The laws of group formation in different social stages are of particular importance.

2) The psychology of national groups: their beliefs, prejudices, likes and dislikes, etc.

3) A science for the renewal of the bases of social life. One could think in this connection of social groups which operate below the state level, such as family groups, face-to-face groups, professional and economic groups, labor unions, etc. All those need a re-orientation in regard to world society as they have been mostly dominated by national and civilisational forms of thought.

In these various trends of thought and theories we find a clear stress on the necessity of viewing international law not as a social institution by itself, but as a science that needs a close contact with social reality in order to fulfil its function. Law has been too much seen as analogous to the law of national states, while it is becoming quite clear that international society will have to be a society based upon cooperation and compromise rather than upon coercion.

International law as a law of compromise will differ from coercive law and has to stand in a much closer relationship to social reality. As is advocated by Alvarez, law in expressing cooperation will function more according to purpose and intent than to the letter. While the days of a purely positivist international law are not over, this law can only function in the interests of world society if it is bolstered by general principles of equity and justice. In this sense, it again needs a natural law foundation.

CHAPTER VI

THE THEORY OF INTERNATIONAL RELATIONS

It is not surprising that the theory of international relations has received considerable attention in the United States. On the one hand, within this country there has been a strong development in political science, while, on the other hand, it has many practical reasons to seek theoretical support for the making of foreign policy.

From the outset it must be remarked that the problem of a theory of international relations is full of epistemological difficulties. Seen abstractly, the relations between states fall within relatively few categories, but as soon as we deal with actual states as groups of people, the possibilities for interaction are practically limitless, while the role of the state in relation to the individual is also extremely difficult to assess as the individual identifies himself with many groups of which the state group is not necessarily the most important one.

If a theory of international relations analyzes international processes empirically, it merely provides a rational scheme for events which have taken place already. If it attempts to analyze change by the methods of trend analysis, it cannot easily get beyond broad generalisations which would not differ very much from current political or historical analyses. An image of the future is essential in the world of politics while a science of international relations can at best contribute to making this image a more rational one, and this would indeed be a very valuable contribution. The expectation which is sometimes expressed that international politics could be manipulated by the aid of scientific theory must be put aside as of small importance because there could be only manipulation of means, but not of goals, and there is nothing new in the manipulation of means.

If the theory of international relations would contribute to a more realistic and rational view of international problems, we could be well satisfied, and there is every reason to enquire how far this process has progressed. This progress is surveyed in two recent publications, "Theoretical aspects of international relations," edited by William T. R. Fox [1] and "Contemporary theory in international relations," edited by Stanley H. Hoffmann.[2]

Stanley Hoffmann begins by pointing out that there is a radical difference between national and international society: the first is regulated by political authority while there is no equivalent of this in international society. "Hence, in particular, the striking differences between domestic and international law, whose elaboration, interpretation and enforcement continue to depend on the will and consent of its very subjects." "Hence also the difference in perspective between the discipline of world politics and "domestic" political science. As one writer has put it, the former begins with the context and is then led to consider the content: its interest is in the environment and in the interrelatedness of everything within; the latter begins within the basic unit and is then led to consider the setting: its interest is in the individual organism and in its relationship with everything without." [3]

Another crucial difference is that international problems are approached with an image that is derived from internal conditions while we have no real international pattern of thought in which the interests of other nations find a place.

The science of international relations can contribute to the emergence of such a mentality which is essential for an ordered world society.

As a definition of this science Stanley Hoffman suggests the following: "The discipline of international relations is concerned with the factors and the activities which affect the external policies and the power of the basic units into which the world is divided." [4] As types of theory, the author distinguishes (1) normative or value theory which postulates certain forms of world society as desirable; (2) empirical or causal theory which analyzes actual political behaviour and identifies the main variables; (3) policy science or theory as a set of recipes for action or as systemic advice for statecraft.

If the author remarks that he does not make a plea for theory for its own sake but considers theory as a set of tools whose usefulness is tested

[1] University of Notre Dame Press, 1959.
[2] Prentice Hall, 1960.
[3] cf. *ibid.*, p. 2. The writer referred to is C. A. W. Manning and his "The University Teaching of Social Sciences": International Relations, Paris 1954.
[4] *Ibid.*, p. 6.

in the solution of concrete problems, one could object that medicine also defines incurable diseases, and that there is no reason to limit theory to what may seem useful at a given moment. In addition, it could be observed that theory mostly combines the aspects of normative, causal and policy theory. In causal theory there is a normative element in what is considered relevant while few theories will arrive at wholly fatalistic conclusions. Theory, it seems, is the art of explaining the obvious from the non-obvious, while it is also a method of ordering our thinking by a system of classification. For instance, if we could explain international tensions as tensions of specific groups within given national societies, we might be putting forth an acceptable scientific theory, but it might not be applicable as the groups in question may refuse the necessary changes. Medicine or criminology are practical sciences because the authority of the state has been put behind them. If this were not so, their findings would be much less easily applicable.

In international relations, illness as well as cure are not so difficult to discover, but there are no ways of utilising the findings, except by persuasion, but in many cases the statesman is bound by an existing set of conditions which limits his choice. In fact, if the objective conditions causing international tensions could be fully determined, this knowledge might be wholly inapplicable.

Let us assume that we conclude that rapid increase of population breeds conflict. This knowledge would not be applicable, unless those in control would be first and foremost concerned about the avoidance of conflict. *If the major concern of the statesmen of the world was to avoid conflict, we would already have a functioning international society.*

If we encourage competition within the states, we also create competition between states, but once competition has reached a certain point, it would take a tremendous psychological effect to reduce it, and we have not seen as yet the emergence of a philosophy by which nations reduce their national efforts for the benefit of world society. We talk about the reduction of armaments, but domination is possible by economic means, by psychic conditioning, etc.

A world society which would be non-competitive requires national societies which are non-competitive, and no prospect of this is in sight, not even on the remotest horizon as even the welfare state is linked to the ideas of international economic competition, just as much as to the ideas of the international spreading of welfare.

These remarks are meant to show that the theory of international relations is not necessarily applicable if it really performs the task of scientific inquiry, namely to explain a situation from causes which seem to be the determining ones. In this way, science is obviously always in a state of flux, but its motivation is constant: it seeks to discover why things are as they are. In some cases, such as medicine, this may lead to the purposive influencing of human behavior; in others, such as astronomy or geology, it does not or only to a much smaller extent.

In fact, one could argue that in regard to theory, international relations might be a relatively simple science, but its main problems are in its applicability, which would only become possible if sufficient individuals, and above all those with a leading function, were to accept a set of principles that does not have to be complex as long as it is rigidly applied.

The simple principle "excessive competition breeds egotism and thereby conflict" could probably be proved empirically in a psychological laboratory. This would pass unnoticed, unless sufficient individuals could be induced to accept the consequences of such empirical findings.

It is worth repeating that in international relations it might be of value to aim for a simple theory and to concentrate on its application. Of all economists, only Adam Smith is generally remembered because he stated a simple principle that was probably not wholly correct theoretically, but it was applicable.

It is a simple theoretical principle that a functioning world society depends upon the self-limitation of the existing states. They must operate within the terms of their own capability, with due regard for the same right of all other states. Power, like a disease, should be isolated before it can be cured, and this means that all states should curb their tendency to power competition and base their national societies upon the principle of normal reciprocal relations with states of comparable capabilities.

There is no true cooperation possible between the strong and the weak, the rich and the poor, but only domination and subordination. Cooperation requires a certain degree of equality, and then it yields normal benefits. We, however, follow the opposite principle which leads to conflict and war: we purposely aim for power and believe that harmony will result from an unknown, imagined source.

The problem of the complexity or simplicity of the theory of international relations deserves some comment.

Stanley Hoffmann is, if not in favor of a simple approach, at least an advocate of a realistic theory. He believes that the study of international relations should begin with the analysis of historical situations. One could think, for instance, of patterns of expansion in different historical periods. The main variables of each system could be identified, and this might be helpful for the analysis of present situations. Another example mentioned is the study of the international behaviour of revolutionary systems which obviously tend to show a certain expansionism. As the only radically new problems of today, Hoffmann mentions those raised by nuclear weapons and those of economic development in a post-colonial phase.

The latter does not seem particularly new, while one misses the mention of increasing world population, the emerging complex, industrialised mass-society and the shrinkage of space for expansion by dominant societies. Important, however, is the insistence upon the study of the relations between basic social units as these not necessarily have to be the national states. Groups above or below the state-level can become the dominant ones, or both those processes can occur at the same time. Another suggestion is the study of foreign policy in periods of waning and of waxing power, and one would be inclined to add, the internal concomitants of this process. The relation between internal and external policies is in general an important field of study as we tend to oversimplify this relationship.

Democratic states have been imperialistic while autocratic states have been self-contained.

It is also of great importance that the study of international problems should be placed within the context of the international system.

"An understanding of world politics, or any aspect thereof, supposes an understanding of the characteristics of the international system. The behaviour of a given variable depends on the kinds of situations or constellations in which it figures, and those situations in turn are largely a function of the international system in which they occur." [5]

In other words, the scientist should attempt to think in terms of a world society as a whole and not in terms of national or bloc interests. Another important aspect is that this study should be dynamic rather than static. We are concerned with the social evolution of mankind as a whole and not with its sub-groups though they have been the basic units of this process.

International relations are no longer an exclusively Western activity but we analyse them in terms of our Western thought-patterns without

[5] *Ibid.*, p. 176.

attempting to see them from the perspective of non-Western civilisations. In addition, there were patterns of international expansion before the period of Western dominance, but we neglect the study of those earlier patterns, for instance, in terms of the relationship between nomadic and sedentary groups. Those patterns could occur anew, but we exclude such possibilities from our thinking.

One can only agree with the following observation: "A return to history would also discourage us from producing explanations in which a determining role is given to a specific variable which happens to play such a role in the present, but did not do it to the same extent at all times; for instance, economic development." [6]

It seems also useful to realize that relations between social groups are always relations between individuals who have been conditioned by their relative groups. When the French army fights the German army, this is not a battle between abstract entities, but a number of individuals, termed French on account of certain attributes, struggling with a number of individuals, termed German for a comparable reason. These individuals have a certain organisational pattern determined by their social group, their own nation, and by the logistics of their task and situation.

In other words, international relations are always relations between individuals, but, at least in political relations, those individuals have a strong national group identification. They have been conditioned to such an extent that they think of the group rather than of themselves, but they are still individuals.

One misses this point in Hoffmann's exposé. He seems to regard the group identification of the individual as a constant rather than as a variable factor. The group allegiance of the individual, however, depends upon the relationship between the individual's life goals and the rewards which the control group (also individuals) offers. If this relationship becomes negative, group allegiance can change very rapidly as is shown by the withering away of apparently stable governments in revolutionary periods.

It might perhaps be very fruitful to see international relations as relations between individuals and to determine what factors influence the identification of the individual with specific groups. Is nationalism, for instance, a conditioned reflex, a genuine emotion or a form of group identification which can be altered by strengthening other groups?

[6] *Ibid.*, p. 177.

For this reason, if one is to study the structure of world society as Hoffmann suggests, the relative intensity of group identification should be added as this is a basic factor. If one were to state that the world consists of a hundred nations, it would be essential to seek to ascertain how intensive the national identification is. Particularly in regard to international conflicts, there is a vast difference between nations with high or low national identification, though a challenge may obviously alter the identification processes.

It is a sound idea to regard world society as a field, but not so much one where groups are the basic units, but one consisting of individuals who identify themselves with certain groups. In this way, international society becomes a function of the consciousness of the individual, and only in this way is there room for improvement, always provided we learn what the determinants of an individual's group identification are. To think in terms of groups introduces a static element because it easily creates the impression that the group identification is a constant factor. If this were so, international society would remain a chaos of national groups, subject to forces of attraction, repulsion and balance, without any rhyme or reason and without any possibility for improvement or rational guidance.

It is not of groups, but of individuals that our world consists, and individuals must strive for improvement by becoming aware of the existence of millions of fellow-beings. Group identification as the dominant factor in the individual's consciousness is the very reason for the non-functioning of world society, or at least wrong group identification. In this way, the study of international relations is part of the science which deals with the processes of our consciousness, rather than a study of groups which appear only as factors in our consciousness. The science of the processes of our consciousness will have to rely more on the exact than the social sciences, though as a science it is only in its beginnings. International is only what appears as such in our consciousness, and it is this very fact upon which we should concentrate our attention.

If a Dutchman buys a package of Chesterfields, this is an international social action. Yet it hardly appears as such in his consciousness. If a Russian makes a space-flight, a Dutch newspaper reader will react to this as an international event because he feels it as a potential threat. The possibility of international conflicts appears in our consciousness, partially because the threat is a reality, but partially because we have been conditioned to react in this fashion.

The two, reality and conditioning, are hopelessly interlinked, and one of the first tasks of international relations is to investigate how this cumulative effect could be reversed.

"Nothing is good or bad, but thinking makes it so" is more true of international relations than of any other human activity. While in regard to national activities, we overstate the rational and understate the irrational, we do exactly the opposite in regard to international affairs. This makes them appear as a "jungle," more so than they are in reality.

If our "optique" of international society were to become more rational and less sensational, this might have a beneficial influence on international affairs themselves and on the mentality of those who conduct them.

Rationality, reasonableness, matter-of-factness, the judging of situations in terms of the qualities of the individuals involved are all qualities for which we strive in relation to events within our national societies. As soon as we come to international events we use stereotypes, emotional judgments, group terminology, etc. whereas it would be logical to use the same categories of thinking and judging as in regard to national events, but even more consciously and intensely as this is more necessary.

There was a similar situation in regard to class thinking, but class thinking in its more emotional forms is now definitely regarded as unconstructive and irrational. This should also hold true in regard to national and bloc thinking, but the culprits are hard to reach and hard to educate.

Our present patterns of thought tend to aggravate international tensions rather than permit them to be seen realistically, and the different reasons for this process are well worth studying. The overprojection seems often to be caused by inner tensions of a psychological, political or economic nature.

In the symposium "Theoretical aspects of International Relations," edited by William T. R. Fox, a number of interesting contributions appear by authors like Paul H. Nitze, Hans Morgenthau, Arnold Wolfers, Reinhold Niebuhr and others, but the contributions remain separate approaches. The concept of power plays a dominant role in several of them, though political power in the twentieth century seems far from being a clear concept.

A highly complex society cannot operate by coercion, and it would seem that the traditional concept of power very much belongs to a society which is already disappearing. This argument seems all the more cogent when one reads Professor Morgenthau's observations about the theory of politics: "what makes a theory of politics possible in spite of the ambiguities of its subject matter is the rationality in which both the mind of the observer and the object of observation, that is, politics, partake. Politics is engaged in by rational men who pursue certain rational interests with rational means."

This overlooks the fact that whatever may seem rational from the viewpoint of national power politics is utterly irrational from the standpoint of world society. Only after goals have been agreed upon, are there rational questions to be solved. The goals themselves, however, belong to a vision of the future which has little or nothing to do with rationality. In fact, a world society is no more rational than the people who compose it, but they may want a world society rather than national power competition. In the same way there is nothing very rational about national societies.

If rationality enters only into means-ends relationships, we become at the same time aware that international relations theory will have to consist of more speculative and analytical than rational and empirical thinking. The desirable society must be visualized; it cannot be read out of the past.

Thus the present theory of international relations offers no more than a vague preliminary stage for a philosophy of world society. It can be a useful tool for understanding the past and may be a means to overcome national or bloc patterns of thinking, but it suffers continuously from a lack of vision and from a deeper understanding of human nature.

CHAPTER VII

THE SOCIOLOGICAL THEORIES

As sociological thinking appears in the form of general thinking about society as well as in the form of more specific theories, it is within these two categories that we must look for approaches to the problems of world society.

In its first stages, sociology was typical of the progress-thinking of the nineteenth century, though it tried to develop a philosophy as well as a method of its own. In the present era, sociological thinking about international problems takes place within the more limited theories that have become customary in modern sociology.

There are not many links between these two types of sociology, and it is better to deal with them in separate sections.

I. THE PHILOSOPHICAL SYSTEMS OF SOCIOLOGY

It was of great importance that the first systems of sociology dealt mainly with the problem of how the process of social evolution must be visualised and how it affects the individual. For the emergence of a functioning world society it is obviously of the greatest importance whether such a stage is seen as the natural outcome of the processes of social evolution. If this is not the case, the emergence of a world society acquires a deterministic quality, and it will come about, quite independently of the volition of the presently living individuals.

It takes, of course, a convinced evolutionist in terms of the exact sciences to proclaim such a theory.

Auguste Comte, the 'father' of sociology, was a social evolutionist, but not wholly of the deterministic type as he believed that rational volition was the most important factor in the evolution of human society. One could observe that the factor of volition has also to be within the context of human capabilities, but seen in this fashion the whole factor of purposive social action becomes an illusion and one can speak only about social action "as if" it were willed or purposive.

Comte, however, did assume that the mutual influencing of people is a factor in social reality which must be taken as such and which can be reduced to an ultimate reason only by speculative thinking, and this Comte considered as superfluous.[1]

Much more modern in his terminology was Herbert Spencer who gave the following definition of evolution "Evolution is an integration of matter and a concomitant dissipation of motion during which the matter passes from a relatively indefinite, incoherent homogeneity to a relatively coherent heterogeneity and during which the retained motion undergoes a parallel transformation." [2]

This definition which, strangely enough, is rarely used nowadays, serves as a useful starting-point while the theory of Spencer about the transition from a military to an industrial society is also worthy of note.

Empirically speaking, the process of social evolution as it has hitherto shown itself has consisted of the gradual emergence of numerically larger and more complex social groups.

In the very long period of preliterate societies, comprising about half a million years we see the trying out of innumerable adaptation patterns by relatively small groups. Only a few of those are apparently fully successful and these lead to the appearance of larger than tribal groups: states, empires, federations of states. The gradual evolution of these groups and their horizontal spreading took place in the period of about 6000 years which we generally term "history." This process is still under way, and it would require a very difficult and complex study to achieve a more accurate picture of this process and its probable further development.

Up to the present time we have had philosophies and scientific theories which developed from enquiries whose focus was specific social groups like states and civilisations, but we have not attempted to combine the available data into a universal science of social evolution, though both the Western and the Communist worlds present such a claim.

The impact of industrialisation on our thinking and the resulting concepts of very rapid social change tend to acceptance of the view that a world society is a matter of an immediate future.

[1] Cf. Littré, "Auguste Comte et la philosophie positive," Paris, 1863. Also Comte's "Philosophie positive."

[2] As quoted on p. 113 in Harry Elmer Barnes Ed., *An introduction to the history of sociology,* University of Chicago Press, Chicago, 1954.

A more balanced view of social evolution would sooner support the contention that the above-described process has not even reached the half-way mark towards a functioning world society.

In the first place, our largest societies, the Western world and the communist bloc, are by no means integrated as yet, while the horizontal spreading of the more complex forms of modern civilisation has barely started and could easily require a few thousand years if one takes into account that the evolution from the tribe to the large industrial nation-state took about five thousand years.

It is erroneous to regard the evolutionary process as a rapid one, and the whole problem cannot be properly discussed unless one first determines by what criterion the speed of social adaptation is measured. If one considers successful survival of the human species as the criterion, then indeed we can speak of rapid evolution, but the time span of this rapid increase has been very short, and we cannot say as yet whether the adaptation of the rapidly growing world population will prove successful and lead to more permanent social forms.

If we take Spencer's definition of evolution and his theory of stages, we are only half-way to the predominance of the industrial society and its deplacement of the military one, while the spreading across the globe of successful adaptation comprises no more than about one third of mankind.

It seems, however, quite impossible to say, unless very complex studies were to be made, what the predictable pattern of complete adaptation would consist of. We have only naive visions of a world state and of a world wide classless society.

In reality, however, a world society could only be very complex and highly structured, and it is possible to arrive at some vision of it only by building up structural theories since social evolution must be seen as a motion towards more structured social forms. It must be borne in mind that "structured" and "centralised" are different concepts which can be contradictory.

The concept of "structure" could be considered as the other important contribution which sociological theory has to offer for the study of international society.

If the two concepts of social evolution and of structure could be woven into one, one would indeed have a theory of development which would be a far more valuable tool than the idea of linear development that dominated the nineteenth century and is still at the back of many of the theories of progress and development.

It is rather strange that while much of the thinking of the twentieth century is deterministic – in the Communist as well as in the Western world – there is nevertheless a great belief in the value of social planning.

Theoretically, the two concepts are contradictory, and there certainly is no justification for regarding social evolution as anything but a natural process.

A natural process can be helped or hindered by purposive human action, but there is no human control over the basic trends of social evolution.

It is mainly due to the preponderance of the exact sciences and to their successful control over natural processes that the idea prevails that human control over social evolution is possible. This leads to the types of deterministic thinking which seriously threaten the continuation of human society.

If one sees social evolution as a process of natural growth, one needs a far more complex theory, but a theory which might be of deeper and more lasting value.

A theory about the natural growth of human society would have to give an image of this process before the question of purposive human social action can even be raised.

If we deal with purposive human social action before we have arrived at a workable theory of social evolution, we may do no more than raise false expectations and unwarranted forms of social thinking.

The theory of natural social evolution points in the direction of more complex and more structured social forms, but it also points to a loss of motion and a decrease in social dynamism, which might come about rather suddenly as most social changes do.

In other words, the theory of social evolution points in the direction of a more stable and permanent world society, with a low rate of change as soon as the processes of social adaptation have reached a workable maximum.

In terms of the individual, this means that a world society would give the individual a feeling of stability and permanence; the exact opposite of the emotions which modern society engenders in the individual.

This again furnishes proof that world society is still a long way off, but that we have to look for its first beginnings where we can find the psychic awareness of the need for a more stable society or for aiming in this direction.

It would seem that the idea of a world state would furnish all that one could wish for in the way of a stable and static society, but the idea of a world state overlooks the need for world society to be visualised as structured and complex, and definitely not as centralised and coercive.

The human being is growing into functional and cooperative behavior-patterns, and the coercion typical of the nineteenth century state is definitely on the way out. In addition, Man is not an animal who lets himself be coerced unless there is a definite reason for it. It is difficult to see what the function of coercion would be in a world society as soon as it had gained a certain permanence.

It is more logical to assume that world society will need structural social groups of the non-coercive type, like family groups, ethnic and regional groups, economic groups, religious groups, regional groups, etc. One should add the state as a functional group, but not as a power group because in this role it definitely hampers the emergence of a world society.

While it is obvious that a world society would need a complex set of rules, these rules should not be seen as analogous to the laws of the national states in the traditional sense, but more as compromise rules, ethical principles, pragmatic behaviorial rules, etc. They would also require different organs and a different ritual and symbolism, in which coercive dispositions from above would play a relatively minor role.

A structured, decentralised social group would need little guidance from above, as it would be realised that all social growth, like all natural growth, has the direction from bottom to top and not in reverse.

The predominance of the coercive state may have stifled the process of normal social growth, and this is perhaps one of the reasons why the coercive state of the nineteenth century is trying to change into the compromise state of the present time.

The process of social growth is one that must be seen as an increasingly collectivist one as the individual identifies himself with increasingly complex groups. His tribal allegiance grows into national allegiance, and the latter into regional, civilisational and also global allegiance, though the latter identification is not strong except in a few cases.

Nevertheless, social growth cannot be seen in terms of an abstractly conceived individual, but only in terms of a social group which increases in size as well as complexity.

This process has been theoretically most adequately expressed in structural theories which stress the interrelatedness of individually appearing factors.

Structural sociological theories have been developed ever since Plato and Aristotle. In the nineteenth century the rationalist versions of the evolutionary theories led to thinking in which the factor "change" took priority over the factor "structure," though in reality both factors are present at all times if we see the evolution of Man as a biological process.

There are no societies without change, nor are there societies without structure as is already implied in the term. As a consequence, one can only speak about differing degrees of change and different degrees of structure, or, if one prefers the term: about degrees of coordination.

As our mind tends to overproject social processes, dynamic periods overstress the factor "change," while static periods overstress the factor "structure."

We have no wholly satisfactory theory which combines the two factors in a theoretically acceptable formula, though it is quite generally agreed that social growth must be seen as a spiralling process, but it is much less clear how we should visualize the transition from simpler to more complex stages. These transitions are often accompanied by violent upheavals, and the process of social change seems to reach a next level abruptly rather than by what we often term an "evolutionary process."

Strictly speaking, however, it is revolution which often appears as the evolutionary process.

It is obvious that the cohesion of the smaller group must be broken before the larger group can appear. This holds also true for the transition from the nation-state to world society.

The difficulty, however, is that social cohesion is not a constant, but a variable. The group allegiance of individuals and sub-groups can alter rapidly, due to structural changes in the larger society.

A national society cannot break up into classes because class groups are incomplete social groups, but a national group can fall back into ethnic, tribal or clan groups or into smaller civil units, such as a province that becomes a smaller separate state.

A world society, if it were to emerge, would consist of a number of subgroups between which the cohesion could be rather low as there is no danger of outer aggression.

The cohesion of a world society would be less than that of a national state of the present time, as the state is a group which responds to internal as well as external challenges. A world society would know the former, but not the latter factor, and this explains to some extent the presently prevailing rather vague fears that a world society would mean a lessening of social cohesion.

This decrease in cohesion gives rise to the fear of a breakdown or a catastrophe, though it should be seen as a social change to which the individual can adjust himself.

If we visualize for a moment world society as having emerged for a brief span of time in its full glory and then as settling down to decentralised forms of life, we see clearly that our present condition could be fairly satisfactory if we viewed it with a different mentality.

The willingness to compromise and coordinate is what makes the emergence of larger groups possible. A dissatisfied or particularly dynamic segment of the old group generally acts as a catalyst, while the required structural change can come about in a number of different ways.

The concept of structure seems to point to the direction of greater structural complexity, but nevertheless with the same basic structural attributes.

The tribe and the state differ in regard to complexity, but not in regard to their basic structural attributes, which arise out of a natural division of labor.

In the same way, a world society will be more complex than the most complex national state, but its division of social labor will still show economic activities, regulatory activities in terms of territorial units and cultural activities (religion, ideology, art and science). The lack of an outer challenge would, however, cause a moderate degree of cohesion, a moderate rate of social change and as a consequence, a different mentality on the part of the individual.

Structural attributes and structural position influence the mentality of the individual.

A private, a captain and a general in an army are conditioned by their relative position within the army structure. An army in battle again has a different behaviorial structure from an army in peacetime.

With a world society the structural position of each individual will differ from that which he holds within a national society. The behaviorial structure of the individual will reflect this difference in position.

Those individuals who adjust themselves to a "role" in a world society are the catalysts of this transitional process, and the world society will exist as soon as a sufficiently large and sufficiently important percentage of the world population identify themselves in this manner and for such a period that these behavior forms become sufficiently stabilized.

As a world society will have a complex structure, it will show a very large number of structural positions and, consequently, considerable differences in mentality, behavior, etc.

The structural position of an individual or a sub-group influences the processes of motivation. Biological and status needs are intermingled in each individual. The more he sees a reasonable chance to gain in status, the more he is willing to make an effort. This principle underlies the competitive society.

In regard to world society, it is active in a somewhat different form. Large countries more easily project themselves into the role of a "large power."

A modern industrial society has proved most successful in large territories with vast natural resources and a moderate population, there is a strong impulse to seek "big power status" if several or at least one of the essential factors is given. Another possibility is the combination of small and medium states into a larger unit in order to achieve the same type of economic-industrial organisation.

If the "natural" factors are not given, the status motive is much less strong. As a result, it is more logical to visualize world society as highly structured and not as egalitarian, though egalitarian types of thinking may correct natural inequalities.

A natural, complex society tends to show focal points of intensive social development, medium points or areas of less intensive social development and a basis of lower development. In this respect, the structure of world society would show similarity to a state without outer enemies, and such a state, like the United States in the nineteenth century, shows considerable social distance, though combined with a spirit of freedom and equality.

As soon as a society gains a certain equilibrium, biological needs gain in significance in comparison to status needs. In a balanced world society production would be geared to consumption, and there is no reason to have excessive expectations about the consumptive needs of the individual if he feels in a stable and permanent position.

For a world society, it is much easier to visualize a closed circuit of production and consumption, but this is impossible with a hundred competing states in which status-needs (military expenditures, etc.) have priority over consumption needs.

The transition from competing national economies to a balanced and durable world economy will be extremely difficult, and the present situation gives little grounds for optimism as the basic problems are not even clearly visualized.

Theoretically speaking, it seems justified to point out that a structural theory and the tenet of structural limitations may prove to be much-needed corrections of one-sided development thinking that is often rooted in political considerations.

II. THE MIDDLE AND SMALL RANGE THEORIES

In sociology a vast amount of work has been done on problems like racial and ethnic tensions, centralised and decentralised groups, political groups, social change, etc. Much of this type of theory will have a bearing on the problems which will emerge in a world society, but the total configuration and general structure of world society will obviously differ from that of national societies.

All present problems will appear in different dimensions and different perspectives.

This makes it logical to expect that new sciences will appear alongside the existing ones, and that there will be a fruitful interaction between the sciences dealing with world society and those dealing with national societies and smaller groups.

The structural difference between the two types of society would be considerable as has been shown above.

For the moment, the general theories of world society and of social evolution are our most pressing need, as the middle and small range theories will only come into focus after they begin to present themselves as such in relation to world society. Sociological investigations of regional development are an illustration of this, but they form a very small percentage of the total output of sociological studies.[3]

[3] Attention is drawn to the *Sociological Bibliographies of Unesco* and to the periodical *Journal of Conflict Resolution,* University of Michigan, U.S.A. This periodical publishes many sociological articles on international problems.

CHAPTER VIII

THE CONCEPTS OF FORMAL AND INFORMAL STRUCTURE

In relation to international society it is more customary to speak about the power and the legal structure, but it may be illuminating to compare these concepts with the sociological ones concerning the formal and the informal structure.

The formal structure of a social group is its structure as conforming to certain legal, moral, religious, ideological, economic, political concepts, etc. and this in relation to reality often means a rationalized or idealized version.

The formal structure is related to what the Germans call the "Ought," while the informal structure is the realm of the "Is."

Those who have a rational or moral version of society have frequently been worried about the conflict between the "Ought" and the "Is." This conflict becomes less alarming if we realize that the concepts of formal and informal structure are both heuristic concepts. In reality, there is only reality.

This means that we are dealing with two visions of reality: the one sees reality as the action-field of rational beings; the other sees Man as an animal who is neither constant, nor rational, but who must be seen in terms of an action pattern that allows him to play a number of roles as long as his energy structure is adequate.

The normal human being can be rational in relation to his work, emotionally attached to a different world, dominated by his imagination in art or in his expectations. A rational vision of Man is incomplete and misleading, though it is obvious that the functioning of complex social groups depends upon Man being "reasonably rational," if this term is permitted.

It would be erroneous, however, to consider our social institutions as rational: neither the economy, nor the legal or political system are rational. The essence lies in their aiming at rationality or pretending to be rational as a status factor or their being satisfied to be pragmatic, practical, authoritative, charismatic, etc. Most social institutions contain a mixture of these motives.

It is only within the context of a sociology of knowledge that an adequate analysis can be given of the interactional process between formal and informal structure, and for the purpose of this study a few general remarks will have to suffice.

While no social institution is rational in the strict sense of the word, there is nevertheless a tension between the behavior patterns demanded by our social institutions and the volition of individuals.

The behavior patterns as they are visualized by those institutions mostly consist of the successful adaptation patterns of preceding generations. This causes also a time-lag between official or formalized behavior patterns and social reality, in addition to the friction between formalized general patterns and individual volitions.

The distance between the two is twofold: the formal structure reflects reactions which belong in a sense to the past while they also formalize human reactions often beyond the degree of normal human behavior.

The distance and the tensions between the formal and the informal structure are one of the mechanisms by which our society operates.

In national societies, the formal structure is a "mixtum compositum" of laws, customs, manners, religious and ethical principles, economic principles, etc. The efficacy of these principles depends upon actual situations and upon the group involved.

Very few events affect a national society in its entirety. Most events cause chain reactions that could be plotted on a structural chart of the society in question and take place in segments of the society.

Within a functioning national society, the tensions between formal and informal structure might almost disappear, particularly if the country in question is small, and if economic conditions are adequate.

For each specific social occurrence, we can indicate what segment of the formal structure and of the social control groups it puts into action and what people are on the receiving end as passive social actors.

In regard to international society the situation is different, because the social actors appear to a much larger extent in the form of government officials, at least in the present time. There are undoubtedly many international social actions upon the economic, cultural, family and other levels, but international society shows a rather hierarchical structure compared to a number of national societies.

The weight of governmental bureaucracies controls practically all social actions, and the control has become much more rigid than in the nineteenth century when international economic action in particular was relatively uncontrolled.

Thus the formal structure of international society consists in the first place of the formalized concepts of international intergovernmental communication in terms of international law and international customs. These same concepts dominate the structure and behavior of the international organizations and their international bureaucracies.

One should add the philosophies of the dominant societies about international society and about its function and future development.

Due to the predominance of governmental bureaucracies, the conceptual arsenal of international society is rather formalized, sterile and static, much more so than in the eighteenth and nineteenth centuries when the social philosophers developed stimulating and valuable ideas. The predominance of positivism in international law has aggravated this tendency.

International society has become the arena in which stereotypes and commonplace thinking predominate. In addition, the distance between formal thinking and the reality of international society is much greater than within the national societies and this often gives an aspect of unreality and futility to international assemblies and international organizations, though through no fault of the actual participants.

Within national societies, there is a system of communications, either formal or informal, between the various levels of society, while in international society there is no developed communications system between the organizational level and the world population.

As a result, the organizational level has become formalized and static while there is no great interest in most countries in international organisation among the people, because the link between the two is a very tenuous one.

International organizations are modelled after national governments, but they represent mostly the executive branches of national governments. As a result, they lack legislative bodies so that the resulting system is weighted far too much in the direction of managerial and executive government.

On the other hand, there is a dearth of thought about the possible forms which a world society might acquire as it could develop quite differently from national states.

In the present situation the choice seems to be between international organizations which become a true world government, regional developments and a cooperative world society that gradually grows out of the existing situation.

There is no road visible leading from the present situation to a real world government so that the choice seems to lie between regional development and cooperation within a structured world society or a combination of those two factors.

In the formal structure of world society, these two, most probable trends are rather underrepresented. The stress upon an egalitarian world society which is unrealistic could easily cause tensions and excessive expectations instead of being constructive.

The present formal structure of world society does not permit of there being any clear location of responsibility. The national official at home and in an international assembly often plays a dual role.

He may genuinely support the ideal of an egalitarian society in his international role, while in his own country he has to fit himself into a much more realistic, political power structure. Or he may give predominance to the national power structure and advocate national goals under the guise of egalitarian ideals.

He has responsibility only to his home group, and to this group he must conform in the long run and on all basic issues. As the home groups generally speaking possess no world ethos, international assemblies move in a vicious circle whence there seems no escape for the time being. They do strengthen, however, an international ethos in those who regularly participate in them, but they may acquire, on the other hand, a rather blurred concept of their own responsibilities.

In the executive field, the contact between international and national bureaucracies has not yet been made the subject of a sociological or psychological study.

Also in this relationship there is a strong dual-role concept. National bureaucracies have considerable influence on the processes of recruitment for international bodies. They tend to keep the best available people in national functions, but, on the other hand the privileged positions with international organisations exert a strong attraction.

Those who occupy the latter tend to form hierarchies and cliques that are strongly change-resisting and aim at expansion. Such expansion, on the other hand, causes resentment and passive resistance on the part of the national bureaucracies.

As a wholly international career is neither possible nor desirable, it would probably be better if international functions would be held only for very restricted periods. This would counteract the trend towards internationalism as a profession, and this is undoubtedly one of the causes of the lack of interest among the world population for international organizations. Their functional significance is often regarded as small, while the "vested interest group" aspect dominates.

The growth of international organizations would only point in the direction of a world government if there were a corresponding decrease in the weight of national government.

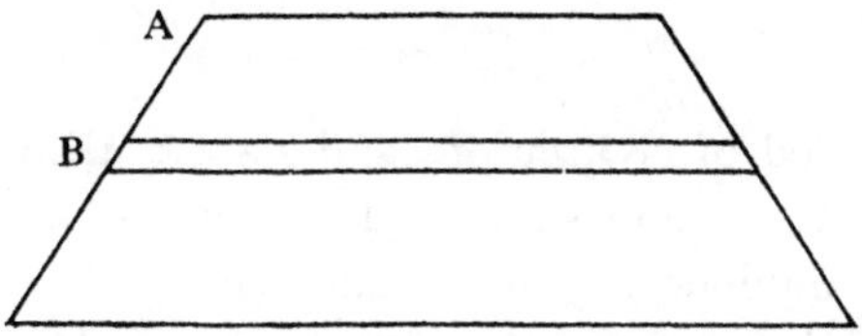

A. Level of world government B. Level of national government

From this diagram, it is quite clear that level A cannot become functional as long as level B is increasing and almost absolute. It does not matter whether level A is seen as authoritative or cooperative, so long as there is no decrease in the weight of level B.

If we have more than a hundred states of totally different power, there is little satisfaction to be derived from defining level A as the common interest of B1, B2, B3, . . . B114, as these common interests are very small unless a moral revolution would take place among national governments so that they would give priority to the interests of mankind as a whole.

Indeed, the whole image of an egalitarian world society based upon the "natural harmony" of individual states is an image derived from the rationalism of the eighteenth century. It has no realistic value in the twentieth century. It may act as a palliative in questions of minor importance, but it also obscures and confuses a realistic view on international society.

If we see social development in terms of the theory of social evolutions, we tend to a different image.

The theory of evolution shows that there was a very gradual and slow development over a period of almost 500,000 years (Phase A: the period of preliterate societies); then a dynamic period of about 6000 years

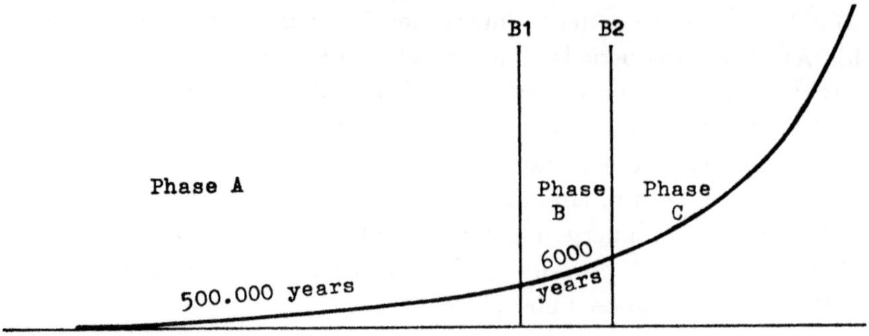

(Phase B: the period of civilizations and states), while finally it would be logical to expect a more static and permanent world society which would endure for millions of years (Phase C).

It is not logical, however, to expect that we are already nearing Phase C, and there is more justification to expect an intermediary phase (second period of Phase B) in which the world civilizations would develop into integrated regional societies, like the United States and Western Europe, the Soviet Union and satellites, Communist China, India, the Arab States and federations in Latin America and Africa.

This would be a far more natural process of growth than the sudden emergence of a world state. This type of thinking is more the thinking of certain groups of Western society in the nineteenth century than realistic or scientific thinking.

It is more likely that we are in the transitional period from phase B1–B2 than in the phase B2–C.

This realisation would require totally different types of thinking about international society and also about the relation between formal and informal structure. While the vision of a future world society should be investigated philosophically as an essential element in our thinking, we should occupy ourselves more directly with the problem of what changes are likely to occur in the near future.

If we are in a transitional stage from the expansionist national state of the nineteenth century towards the regional integrated state or groups of states of a common civilisational type of the twentieth century, we have a number of questions that acquire a different aspect.

The national Western state as it developed from 1600 to 1918 was organised via class groups which were internally antagonistic and externally expansionist. These are two interrelated aspects of a dynamic social group which cannot be internally harmonious and externally expansionist. The seeking of new adaptation patterns – political, economic, technological, etc. – cause class friction as well as the desire for external expansion in order to demonstrate the superiority of the newly found adaptation patterns over those of other groups.

The expansion of Europe was undertaken by class groups: the territorial rulers pursued territorial conquests; the merchants the establishment of trading companies and trading posts; the industrialists control over raw materials and cheap labor; the financiers the possibilities of investment. This expansion largely took place without major wars outside Europe, but it caused the national wars of Western powers whose leading groups jealously watched the expansion of related groups in other nations.

Without the dynamism within the states, the expansion would not have been possible.

The internal situation of the leading states of the twentieth century is totally different: they have become more integrated and are controlled from above instead of by the dynamism of class groups. They also have become economically more self-sufficient. In addition their inner social complexity has become so much greater that international conflict tends to upset or destroy the fabric of the modern superstate.

For these reasons there would seem to be much less reason for conflict between the regional states or groups of states of the twentieth century than there was in the preceding century.

The value of power has altered: the conquest of land as such is not a motive, nor the predatory war as the leading nations are already too rich rather than too poor; the need for raw materials is also less for the modern superstate, while cheap labor is of no value in a highly integrated and complex economy.

If the world were seen in terms of six to seven powerful groups, the existing problems could find easy solutions. We approach, however, the problems of the twentieth century with the mentality of the nineteenth, and this unfortunate situation is used to great advantage by frustrated nations which still project themselves in their role of the nineteenth century, though they pay lipservice to regional and global arrangements.

The new world structure has to be accepted in order to be real: we must accept the power of America and Western Europe, of the Soviet Union and its satellites, of Communist China, of India and of Several other areas which have a chance to gain in power status. None of those groups are interested in an egalitarian world society and a world government; nor are they eager for war as war would serve none of their purposes.

This means that our forms of international thinking should undergo certain changes: we should accept the regional and emerging large states as the focal points of world power. This reality should be expressed globally, for instance, in the Security Council and the General Assembly of the United Nations, but, far more important, we should develop regional and interregional organisations and reduce the weight of formalistic global organisations.

A Western Council of Wise Men meeting comparable councils from other regions might achieve far more than large assemblies, extended meetings, etc. where those who are most directly concerned can never even come to grips with vital issues.

Again disarmament is much more an interregional than an international problem, and it should be dealt with only by states of sufficient power status.

The recognition of natural regional interest spheres would go a long way towards the abolition of conflicts. Most conflicts are not about colonial or non-colonial matters, but about the recognition of regional interest spheres. The regional state or group of states should basically limit itself to its own region.

Most existing conflicts are about this problem, and several others are already emerging on the horizon. They are met with nineteenth century concepts, like self-determination, non-aggression, stability, vested interests, etc., but they are not met realistically.

One shudders when one realizes that an atomic war could break out about these secondary problems, and yet the possibility is there as long as we continue to use the outmoded international tools of the nineteenth century.

The modern superstate feels no need to embark upon either conquest or expansion, but it fears that another emerging superstate will not share this feeling.

A permanent conference of world regions could do much to ameliorate this situation.

The global level needs simplification; the regional level development, but not in the way of the formalistic legal structures of the nineteenth century, though they are better than none.

Let us try to recapitulate: the theory of social evolution points to an intermediary level of regional organisation rather than to the emergence of a world society in the foreseeable future.

The idea of a world society as a world state has been the result of the state thinking of the Western world. At present it is neither realistic, nor applicable.

The greater likelihood of a new world structure, based upon regional groups, needs to be processed in our international thinking and to be transformed into new forms of international organisation.

Many can be devised: regional councils as the basis of world organisation; regional councils alongside global organisations, but interlinked so that there is a dualism of rules; a certain weighting of states in global organisations after this has been accepted regionally, etc.

There are many ways of making the formal structure of world society more realistic, once we have recognized the need for this. But if the tensions between international forms of thought and international reality continue to be excessive, those tensions themselves will be a contributory cause of world conflict. And this is a heavy responsibility.

CHAPTER IX

THE REALITY STRUCTURE OF WORLD SOCIETY

The reality structure of world society is commonly designated as the "power structure," and this is in itself symptomatic, as it indicates the excessive weight that the term "power" has acquired in our thinking. There are many forms of power: spiritual power, the power of knowledge, power of will, physical power, hypnotic power, but "power" has come to mean in the first place the capability of the state to use armed might.

From the point of view of an emerging world society, this power is as atavistic as the club of the caveman, but it is unfortunately the dominant factor in contemporary world society. Perhaps one should see it as a latter-day hypertrophy of an outdated social form which is kept artificially alive by overstressing it.

While military power had a political function in the past, it has nowadays less of a national political function, but it has been transferred to the power bloc, which can either become the nucleus of a regionally organized world society or mean the disintegration of the nation-state.

Particularly because the power-bloc has not been formalized in our international thinking, it has all the elements of an emerging social group, which generally exists first as a vital force, before it takes on formal characteristics. As long as the power bloc is visualised as a superstate, it has the disadvantages of a state and none of the advantages of a regional and self-contained society. It is a hybrid form which uses the power means of the national states of the nineteenth century in a millionfold magnified manner, while it has no reason to do so, as it is relatively self-sufficient, and has no real need for excessive offensive or defensive armaments.

An additional drawback is that modern nuclear armaments are by nature more offensive than defensive. This would make their gradual abolition an essential concomitant in the transition from this power bloc to the integrated regional society.

This transition is the crucial problem of our time. The power bloc is as much an anachronism as a possible tool for the future. To abolish it by returning to a system of really independent individual states is difficult and seems to contradict the natural trend towards larger social groups in terms of economic and social organisation. It is equally difficult to visualise a transition from a bipolar social structure to a universal state or a system based upon an accepted hegemony of one state.

This leaves the alternative of formalising and functionalising the regional structure and making it into a multipolar instead of a bipolar system.

Raymond Aron in his "Paix et Guerre entre les Nations" [1] demonstrates very convincingly that any functioning social system has to be multipolar as a bipolar system lacks a stabiliser and leads to unlimited power competition.

The present world offers a frightening example of this. "The stabilising influence of the non-aligned countries is clearly noticeable, though functionally under-developed. In the United Nations it occurs often that the voting does not take place in terms of the power blocs, but, for instance, in terms of regional groups or of underdeveloped versus developed." [2]

The whole terminology has become distorted, however, by the overstress on power, often considered synonymous with development, and the functionalisation of the power blocs would also lead to a different philosophy about the structure and further development of world society.

The functionalisation of the power blocs and the development of additional regional societies could be accomplished at short notice. In the first place, a lessening of tensions between the power blocs could lead to a decentralisation of groups within those blocs, like, for instance, a Western and an Eastern European Federation of States.

Secondly, either large countries or groups of countries could be given the security function for a certain region. This could apply to China, India, the Arab League, emerging federations within Africa and in Latin America.

A regional security system could be brought within and coordinated by the United Nations, while the armaments of the regional security powers would be determined functionally.

This would lead us out of the deadlock on armament and disarmament

[1] Paris, Calmann-Lévy, 1962.

[2] Cf. Bloomfield.

between the superpowers and point clearly in the direction of arms control. As a regional security system would be multipolar, it would create the functionalisation of needed military power. Thus it would end the nightmarish and cataclysmic process of "escalation" which seems to lead to a "doomsday society," even if the threat never materialises. In any case the armaments race makes a functioning world society impossible.

As the arms race came out of bipolar power competition, it can best and most quickly be solved by multipolar functionalisation of the world's security system. This might also be the most rapid "de-escalation" process.

This could be visualised in detail as follows:

1) The power blocs acquire the status of regional security systems within the framework of the United Nations.

2) The superstates within the power blocs reduce their nuclear armaments to a functional level. The superstates, having superior nuclear force, could accept a unilateral reduction as a moral gesture which would undoubtedly give more prestige than would a further increase in armaments.

3) The borders of the security regions are established by mutual consent and confirmed by the United Nations.

4) The security function within the regional security systems is decentralised and transferred to regional groups or individual nations. These groups or individual nations have only conventional arms.

5) Other regional security systems are formed. The nations establishing them agree to refrain from all nuclear armaments.

6) The regional security system is under supervision of the Security Council, consisting of representatives of the security regions.

7) The latter body gradually reduces all nuclear armaments until they are abolished entirely. As soon as the system becomes stabilised, there is less urgency about the time factor.

In this way, the most dangerous level of world society, viz. the bloc-level would be functionalised so that world society would have four interlinked social levels:

1) The global organisations.

2) The bloc security system, to be strengthened also economically, culturally, etc.

3) The regional organisations.

4) The individual states.

The advantages of this system would be manifold:

a) There would no longer be the excessive gap between formal and informal structure. The organisational superstructure would be "real" in terms of the power structure.

b) The relationship between the two superstates would be functionalised. Their military power would be determined upon the basis of a regional security function, not purely in relation to each other.

c) The small and medium nations of the world could press for these arrangements in the United Nations without being disloyal to their "protectors."

d) The populations could support such a scheme because it would not radically alter the existing status structure.

e) It is realistic and constructive, and would make a further development possible without altering the balance of power.

f) Mankind has a right to be freed from the threat of nuclear devastation, and in this way the nuclear powers can recognize this right upon a functional basis.

g) One of the stumbling blocks of arms control is the insistence upon technical parity. A functional parity would be more feasible, and would be less difficult, bearing the sensitivenes of the superstates in mind.

h) The political hegemony of either superstate is no longer a legitimate goal, and under a functional system the medium and small powers could no longer be drawn willy-nilly into the sphere of power expansion.

i) If armaments are functionalised, there will be an end to the unfortunate interaction between national power goals and economic interests. The economy will have to adjust itself to serving the needs of mankind upon a normal basis. Economic overexpansion is almost as much a danger as the striving for political hegemony.

The scheme outlined above not only fits in with ideas on arms control, but it takes them out of the atmosphere of bipolar power competition. It is this bipolar and unregulated power competition which threatens mankind, and as mankind has not enough direct power to prevent this power conflict, the first step would be to bring it within the orbit of functionalised social relationships.

The idea of a balance of power alone is not enough, as the dynamism of economic and technical development tends to upset this balance at any given moment. It must be put within the context of an organisational system that is more realistic than the present structure of the United Nations, or that could be added to it.

The balance of power system worked in less dynamic periods but it cannot operate without purposive control if the internal conditions of countries show a high degree of dynamism. The inner dynamism makes the international situation unstable, and this results in the automatic control systems of preceding centuries no longer being operative.

The same phenomenon prevails in relation to arms control: the speed of technological innovation makes the idea of technical parity unrealistic and again it is always met by the major nations with suspicion or used to implement specific goals.[3] If the parity were to be functional rather than technical, it would be transposed into an effort to build up a social system of which a certain amount of trust is an innate attribute. No factory could be run if we had to assume that the workers were purposively trying to disrupt the production process; nor could any state exist if all citizens were to distrust all other citizens. Control is only a corrective mechanism in an already functioning social system.

A system based upon mutual terror is not a social system as it prevents normal social growth on both sides and leads to escalation and accumulation of the means of terror.[4] This means that the idea of mankind as a world society is wholly absent as a motive force because otherwise such developments would be clearly impossible.

They fall entirely within the realm of national power politics in a period and in a world situation in which the ideas of political power, of hegemony and of power expansion have already lost their functional significance.

They are obviously distorted over-projections of power which find their root more in the internal conditions of various countries than in a realistic evaluation of the possible further development of world society. This society is now in a rudimentary stage while its further growth is blocked by power politics whose participants strive for spheres of influence rather than for any real international coordination, even in the more limited regional sense, while the effort of coordination is almost wholly absent upon the global level.

This situation must be recognized and diagnosed as such, before it can be ameliorated. Stabilisation of the respective spheres of influence is

[3] Cf. Bechneefer, Berhard G., *Postwar negotiations for Arms Control,* The Brookings Institution, Washington, D.C., 1961; also Becunan, Donald G. (ed.), *Arms Control, Disarmament and National Security,* George Braziller, New York, 1961. The idea of regional security systems is dealt with by P. M. S. Blackett in *Studies of War,* Oliver & Boyd, Edinburgh and London, 1962, and in Strachey.

[4] Cf. Kahn, Herman, *On the thermonuclear war,* Princeton University Press, Princeton, N.J., 1961.

preferable to the danger of further expansion, whether this expansion is planned or haphazard. In either case, it involves the danger of a world catastrophy, which is wholly unjustifiable in terms of mankind as a whole.

The concept of political power is as outmoded as the concept of economic power as a means of control by people over people. Also the idea of economic expansion must be curtailed, internally as well as externally, if it is not geared to the needs of mankind and built upon a worldwide system of production and consumption, with as little excessive development in certain areas as possible. In addition, from the point of view of a world society, agriculture has priority over industry, while at present the opposite is true. Also in this respect, stabilisation will have to precede coordination and even the idea of stabilisation in terms of regional systems is at present almost absent.

Permanence and expansion are contradictory concepts. There is mostly room for economic expansion in areas where there is insufficient production in terms of the needs of the population. The power economy, on the other hand, needs to be purposively curtailed in order to reach a functioning economy which serves mankind as a whole.

As the role of regional development is seen alternatively either as a means by which one of the power blocs can attain hegemony or as a "natural" development in terms of economic and technical trends, it leads to confused forms of thinking. Regional developments, like those in Western Europe, which aim at increasing rather than decreasing the social distance between various parts of the world are negative rather than positive. They have a hegemonistic undertone.

It should be kept in mind that the status difference which came out of the class struggle of the nineteenth century has been transferred to the international level. The state of the nineteenth century was the equal of other states.

The ideological conflict of the twentieth century has given rise to a status difference between states which is unfortunate and which strengthens the role of the ideological blocs. They both attribute a "mission" to themselves, which is a form of expansionism but each considers its own expansion as a natural right or as a form of progress while it labels the expansion of the other side as "aggression."

In this way, both sides attempt to introduce value-judgments into their bloc policies while these should really be seen as the policies of expansionistic states which attempt to line up their respective allies for hegemonistic policies.

A clear recognition of the power blocs as groups of states of equal value would considerably ameliorate this condition. It is not possible to approve economic expansion and to condemn political expansion though the first form might be more bearable and even offer certain advantages to the people. The difference is, however, one of degree: economic expansion leads to growing political influence, as is evident in the relationship between the United States and Western Europe, while political domination is presented as a shortcut to economic progress, though this picture is certainly often unrealistic and onesided.

The common denominator of economic and political expansion is expansion as such, and it is expansion as such which should be regulated and curtailed upon a regional basis.

The motion should be from a hegemonistic world system towards a balance of power system, which needs to be formalised and functionalised. This places the greatest moral burden upon the major countries as they must purposively curtail their hegemonistic tendencies and restrict their own power in the interests of mankind as a whole.

As a certain missionary zeal has often been noticed in the American attitude, a more idealistic purpose for American society should not be considered impossible, though it clashes with the unrealistic idea of continued economic expansion which stimulates egotism and prevents cultural values from coming to the fore.

Man is capable of building purposively a superstructure upon the basis of power relationships, and this is what "culture" should really mean: the conscious creation of interhuman relationships upon a higher level, which accords the individual greater security, greater permanence and full development of his spiritual, artistic and moral attributes. Economic expansion can destroy all cultural values if it goes beyond a certain level. The creation of useless commodities is a play-form of culture which is without great real significance and which has little or nothing to do with the elevation of the individual in his interhuman relationships.

If the dominant nations had fully developed culture systems, it would be impossible for world society to be in a state of scientific neo-barbarism, as even primitive tribes had often a higher cultural level than present-day world society as a whole. The fact that it finds itself in a condition of pathological barbarism must be attributed to a lack of cultural values within the nations, which are unable to see Man as an individual, but which are hypnotised by the power potential of mass societies, which are kept in a condition of tension by the fear of economic or political expansion or aggression from the other side.

In reality, they are self-sufficient, and they could strive for the development of flowering cultures. There is every reason for world society to be ashamed of its lack of any cultural achievements: its potentiality is higher than that of former periods which should make us aware of the low level of our present period.

It is quite evident that the building of a world society and of a world culture has to be preceded by a stabilisation of the political conditions of the present.

There are three dominant views about the political forms of a world society: there are the hegemonists, who believe in the dominant control of one power. They are outmoded in their thinking and they should be seen as the reactionaries of the twentieth century.

In the second place, there are the balancists who believe that a balance of power system could come out of the present hegemonistic struggle between the United States and the Soviet Union. This balance of power system could be most realistically seen as a regional balance of power system rather than as one between states. This view has been argued in this study. A regional balance of power system could be built upon a purposively built regional security system which would put an end to interregional and unregulated power competition.

The "balancists" are the "Realpolitiker" of the twentieth century and their ideas could be implemented at short notice.

Finally, there are the "mondialists' who desire the transition toward a world society within a brief period. They are the progressives who are represented by jurists, advocating a world state, by theologians and moralists, arguing for a world community, and by socialists and communists who desire a world economy geared to the individual and functioning, after an initial planned stage, almost automatically.

The three groups are represented in all countries of the world. Our future requires the unmasking of the hegemonists as such; the rapid stimulation of the balancists' viewpoint and a clearer formulation of its policies; an increase and extension of the role of the mondialists as the vanguard of the future.

Between these viewpoints every individual can choose and accept his full responsibility. The hegemonists are the enemies of Mankind, as much as the balancists and the mondialists are its friends. As our future depends upon the dominance of common human values, the choice is not difficult to make. It requires, however, that we regard "the others" as our equals and that we abandon all ideas of superiority in whatever form they may occur. The building of the future is the common concern of all of us.

CHAPTER X

THE FORMAL STRUCTURE OF WORLD SOCIETY

The formal structure of world society is largely a legacy from the nineteenth century, and, more specifically, of its legal and governmental types of thinking.

It is based upon the tacit assumption that a world society will assume the form of a world state. In the Western world, this hypothesis is rarely questioned, but it nevertheless deserves close scrutiny.

If we consider the reality structure of world society, we find more than a hundred states with vast differences in power, population, area, resources, social systems, ideologies and beliefs, etc. These states could also be classified into groups consisting of those which are more or less satisfied with the status quo, those which have acquired considerable power in the recent past and those which still project their own power into the future, mostly conceived as a very near future in terms of time.

The power expansion of states has been generally in terms of vertical as well as of horizontal growth. The term "vertical growth" means that greater power is often derived from a more complex division of social labor while "horizontal growth" means that powerful states have a tendency to extend their power over other peoples and over available territories.

The rate of expansion is a function of state capability and room for expansion: vertical, in terms of technology, social organisation, urbanisation, etc. and horizontal, in terms of the possibility of political and/or economic expansion, measured against the risk and costs involved.

The idea that the processes set off by these forces could be controlled by a world government seems to avoid the most essential questions. The first is how a world government could arise out of the present situation; secondly, whether a world government can be devised that would effectively control over three thousand million people, and, thirdly, how such a government could function effectively.

The main problem which is basic to all those questions is whether it is justified philosophically to assume that a world society would acquire the form of a world state.

It seems clear from the very start that a world society would only require internal organisation as it would not be faced with the possibility of attacks from the outside. For this very reason it could not be compared to the present states which have the function of internal as well as external organisation.

A functioning government with only internal functions is conceivable, but it could only exist if there were a global division of labor, a world citizenry and a sense of belonging to mankind as a whole.

There is no such "species feeling," not even in the animal world, as groups of human beings are oriented in terms of their habitat and its expansion from a point which is considered as central.

Mankind consists of groups which are growing *toward* each other, not *with* each other, and for this reason each group feels the growth of other groups as a menace.

This explains why the idea of a world government has been mostly favored by nations who are interested in the status quo. They want to combine with other powers in order to forestall or check the growth of other nations.

Such arrangements are, however, no step toward a world government, because a world government would be only acceptable to the majority of Mankind if it would not be an impediment to its further growth and development.

This growth is always uneven, and because of this fact the people project themselves with the group which corresponds to their innate dynamism. This group is not always a state; it can be and has been a political party, an ideological group, a religious group, an economic group, etc.

The formal division of the world into states does not alter these processes and makes it even more difficult to detect them. It would be more essential to divide mankind into highly dynamic, reasonably dynamic and more static groups. Those terms must be understood not in absolute, but in relative terms: increasing or decreasing power in relation to other groups.

These groups play a different role within different states. If the dynamic groups within a state dominate, we tend to designate this state as dynamic. In the same sense, we can speak about reasonably dynamic and static states.

The idea of a world state has been generally favored by the groups within national societies which are anxious for a stable world society: groups which are satisfied with the status quo, groups which aim for more acceptable forms of expansion, groups with moral and religious motives, etc.

As far as the state groups are concerned, the reasonably dynamic and static states desire a certain measure of world government as a means by which to restrain the highly dynamic states. The first – and this is crucial – do not desire world government as such, but they desire the degree of world government which corresponds with their own wishes.

This explains the floating character of world government and international agencies: they represent certain interests of certain states at a certain time.

This, however, is not what the term "government," viz. to "govern" really means, and in this sense there is no world government, nor are there many supporters for a world government, quite apart from the technicalities involved.

A world state would require a world people, a worldwide division of labor and a world government.

None of these factors are given, and it cannot be reasonably expected that they will develop within a favorable future.

Before social groups can merge, they must coexist and cooperate for a long time. In addition, it seems erroneous to assume that the coercive powers of national governments could be transferred to a world government.

National governments use the threat of coercion against individuals, classes and sometimes regional groups which are already part of an existing social structure.

If we observe that a considerable part of Mankind is dissatisfied with the status quo, it seems obvious that coercion is not a tool that could be used by a world government. In addition, coercion by outside and strange agents would be felt as an insult by the majority of the people of the world.

To offset these difficulties, the idea of a world government is presented as an ameliorative agent which would guide and plan social progress.

If the desire for progress lives within people, they can bring it about, and international aid for this purpose is most constructive.

The highly dynamic groups, however, do not strive purely for economic development: they strive for power, and power desires could not be regulated by a world government, unless they were to find a formulated and functionalised expression.

This, however, is in the first place a strategic and psychological problem as power changes quite logically involve power gains as well as power losses, because power is a relative concept.

We do not doubt that nations accept power gains, but do they also accept power losses?

This problem could be solved only by a totally different mentality which would view the state as a functional social group which can grow, be rather stable or diminish in power.

This mechanism has operated with the tool of war, but we cannot solve it by ignoring it. In addition, it is very doubtful whether power is a transferable quality.

Power is the result of human strength, and this strength cannot be simply transferred to other human beings, just as we cannot transfer intellect or talent.

This becomes clearer if we accept that in contemporary world society the power of nations is largely determined by their industrial strength. This industrial strength of nations cannot be transferred: it is a given fact though this strength is not a constant, but a variable factor. It is certain that most nations are striving to acquire this industrial power; we do not know, however, whether they will succeed as we have no way of measuring their strength, in regard to the future, as other nations are also acquiring this type of power.

The evolution toward industrial society is the factor which most of mankind of our period has in common. This evolution has a twofold face: industrial society is viewed as a means of attaining power and as a means of satisfying the basic desires of the world population.

The methods for reaching the industrial society are mainly two: the gradual evolution which the Western world advocates and the forced evolution within a short time span for which communism and its centralized techno-bureaucratic control regards itself as the method par excellence. The more retarded in the evolution towards the industrial society a country is, the more it tends to stress the power goals, particularly if it consists of a vast territory, and a large population, while the consumptive goals belong to a later stage of evolution.

Neither the Western, nor the Communist world present a clear picture of how a fully developed global industrial society would look.

Both of them are dynamic, though they present different stages in the evolutionary process: the West, and particularly the United States, could make the attempt to transform the overly dynamic industrial society into a more permanent, more livable and more diversified social form, while the Communist world has not yet reached the point where the problem of the final and more permanent form of industrial society has to be met philosophically or practically.

If we ask ourselves the question what the formal structure of a functioning world society would look like, we have to take into account the transition from the predominantly political society of the nineteenth century towards the predominantly industrial society of the present time and the future.

The formal structure of world society has been inspired mostly by the forms of that political society, and it is slow to adjust itself to the demands of the industrial society.

Yet there is a considerable cleavage between the social forms of these two types of society. The political society is centralized, coercive, atomistic and based upon an abstractly conceived individual who does not exist in social reality.

Industrial society tends to become more decentralized if not motivated by power considerations; it cannot operate by coercive controls, but is cooperative in character; it has to be conceived of as a whole if it is seen functionally; it is based upon functional groups rather than upon the individual.

Not only in regard to forms, but also in regard to social techniques, the two types of society are different. The social techniques of political society are authoritative, rational and formalistic; the techniques of industrial society are based upon a social compromise and upon the structural concepts of organization, and are psycho-sociological instead of legal in their ultimate orientation.

The state demands; the industrial society structures. The state threatens; the industrial society promises. The state directs itself at rational Man; the industrial society at the human being as a compositum of drives and impulses. The state educates via the conditioned reflex; the industrial society imparts technical skills, social techniques, and ultimately, the use of the freedom of the affluent society.

It is the dilemma of our times that we find ourselves in the transitional stage between the two societies: the political society warps and distorts the industrial society; the industrial society stimulates outdated desires for political power which may acquire pathological forms.

What world society needs is not so much organisations, all geared after the political society, but a philosophy which makes it clear that we find ourselves in a process of social evolution which is worldwide, and neither Western, nor communist, but a motion towards new social forms which may retain some of the attributes of our present world, but to which new ones wil be added.

It is not a problem of power that we are facing, because power is outdated, but the problem of finding the social forms which give a lasting framework to industrial society in its various stages of evolution and geared to its ultimate and more permanent form as the directive principle.

Power means direct and complete control of human beings over other human beings. The authoritative person is formalistic, cold, he threatens directly or indirectly. For him there is no place in the industrial society which is by nature based upon cooperation towards a common goal. The power state does not know a common goal: its lust for power, for conquest, for expansion are the attitudes of certain classes of the political society of the past. They were functional in a past stage of social evolution, but they have become a menace, a hindrance to the emergence of a global industrial society.

It ought to be the international organisations which show development towards these new social forms: they are cooperative, and not coercive, though they still formulate the latter as their goal.

It is not a realistic or a functional goal, and they could make a virtue out of their present weakness by seeking to grow into cooperative social forms instead of political ones.

The need for this has been acknowledged: the Economic and Social Council of the United Nations, Technical Assistance, etc. are half-hearted acknowledgements of the primacy of global social evolution towards a society which we should visualize more fully.

By ignoring power, we shall conquer power as the mechanism of social control for which it is no longer fitted.

The functionalisation of international organisation would require: 1) universality; 2) weighted and functional representation; 3) additional functional organizations.

1. *Universality.* There seems to be little or no cogent reason to argue the need for universality of the United Nations. It is rather convincing proof that the political orientation dominates that universality has not been reached up to the present time.

The "universality" of social reality – if the use of this term is permitted

– is obvious because what it is. If we think of world society in terms of the industrial society, it would seem very awkward to ignore vast groups of producers and consumers who, in addition, identify themselves with national power goals.

As those latter goals are linked to industrial capability, it would be most natural to desire a certain regulation of those capabilities and their growth via international agencies.

Only outdated political conceptions can overlook this by ignoring unregulated power capability and its changes and by regarding states as predominantly political groups which are no longer a social reality.

Even politically the technique of non-recognition seems a painful remnant of the period when foreign policy was the prerogative of certain classes. "Nice people ignored not-so-nice people." As this has not prevented the changes within our societies, it seems strange to apply such a technique to the complex processes of world society which deserve to be taken even more seriously than our internal problems. Inside our national societies we no longer ignore what we do not like.

The bewildering conclusion is again that our thinking about foreign problems is *behind* our national thinking, and not in advance of it. Progress, mostly in terms of technological development, has shown a considerable impact on the social techniques of our national societies, but it has had little or no impact on world society.

The best example of this is perhaps that while increased technical power is used for social control within our societies, which are based upon compromise, internationally industrial capability has led to the emergence of the "threat society."

The "threat society" tries to reach political goals by threatening total nuclear annihilation. Do employers and workers within our national societies threaten one another with annihilation before arriving at a compromise?

The techniques of coercion of the political society have led to the proliferation of technical means of coercion. Within our societies, the industrial evolution has made physical coercion obsolete; internationally, the industrial revolution has worsened political conflicts.

It is useful, however, to reflect that there is no stringent relationship between social techniques and means of physical coercion. Even the "threat technique," however primitive it is, can take place upon various levels of technical capability. The "overkill capability" is the result of the unregulated growth of industrial societies.

It is this problem that international organisation should seek to solve upon a realistic basis, and it should be accorded the highest priority.

2. *Weighted and functional representation.* It is here that the contrast between the social techniques of the political and the industrial society is most salient.

The political society thinks in terms of political entities, abstractly conceived as equal and given equal legal status. It sees world society as atomistic coexistence of sovereign and equal states, possessing the fictitious right of self-determination. These forms of thought make a functioning world society practically impossible.

The industrial society thinks in terms of dynamic social groups living within a certain territory. The "weight" of these social groups is determined by their capability. The interrelationships between these societies are dynamic and can be mathematically expressed in order to have a suitable basis for compromises. The industrial society is relatively self-sufficient and not interested in expansion against heavy odds. The interrelationships between those societies should be seen as matters of give-and-take and not upon the basis of absolute principles.

Weighted voting with the possibility of adjustment in relation to capability changes, would be the proper form of international organisation for this type of transitional stage between political and industrial society.

3. *Additional functional organisations.* The same train of thought could be continued in regard to political and functional forms of international organisation. It is obvious that the political society favors parliamentary assemblies, the idea of a world legal order, a system of collective security, the idea of total and complete disarmament within the framework of the United Nations, and finally, the creation of a central agency for coercive control over inter-nation conflicts.

The industrial society, on the other hand, operates in the direction of functional organisation. Organs of an economic nature, but politically organised, can be regarded as a hybrid form. The latter designation seems justified because they are based upon the idea that a coordinated economy upon a satisfactory level is essential to world order but they seek the realisation of this idea via agencies that are organised in the conventional political manner.

Functional organisation can be seen in two ways: it leaves a specific function within the framework of the state, but it seeks an organisational form which takes into account the interests of various social groups and not only of the state as such.

A second possibility is to lift a given activity out of the framework of state control and to place it directly under the supervision of an international agency. The most important example of this was the Baruch Plan at the end of the Second World War which sought to place all nuclear materials directly under an international agency. Unfortunately, this attempt failed because it would have prolonged the nuclear monopoly of the United States for the transitional period during which the agency would not yet have come into existence.

Whether it is possible to lift a certain activity out of the framework of the state and to place it under internationalised functional control is a complex problem. The European organisations obviously confirm this possibility, but the functionalisation in this case refers to the common interests of a small number of states which are already similar in many respects and which have economies that were interrelated for many centuries. In addition, their power of international decision-making had been severely curtailed by the North Atlantic Alliance, which also welcomes the more geographically limited forms of integration of the Six. The functional integration could therefore be regarded as an outcome of political integration and not wholly in terms of the need for a superstructure of the industrial society.

If we were to regard the industrial society as a regional one, this would lead to different forms of international organisation. In the first place, there would be the organs of the regional industrial societies, like the European organisations, Comecon, the Latin American common market, the Arab League, etc. These organisations are, however, neither universal, nor is it clear whether they should be regarded as political or functional. In the second place, there is no system to coordinate the regional organs. They are competitive instead of cooperative.

The transitional stage from the political to the industrial society is clearly reflected in our forms of international organisation. If it is admitted that functional organisation is only possible upon the basis of common interests, it is obvious that a political understanding in terms of a balance of power policy or in terms of far-reaching coordination is the essential prerequisite.

"Co-existence," which describes the present relationship between East and West, cannot lead to any functional form of organisation, for instance, in regard to armaments, because the realm of common interests is not sufficiently developed and too fluid to permit any institutionalisation.

An international nuclear policy organ, for instance, consisting of the nuclear powers would be most useful, but we find no such organ. An international steel or oil council or an organ for the preservation of the world's resources or for the utilisation of the oceans has been suggested by several groups like the Pugwash Conferences on Science and World Affairs, but in spite of some beginnings like the Geophysical Year, there has been little progress.

Functionalisation has only proved possible where political power interests are not involved, but it has not been utilized extensively in order to reduce power competition. An exception could be made for the Technical Assistance rendered by the United Nations, but these developments have been slow and often rather disappointing because they are ultimately utilised within the framework of political interests.

Real although limited cooperation between East and West is the absolute requirement for functional organisation upon a global level. As long as this factor is not given, functionalisation as an inner-region activity may aggravate inter-regional tensions.

CHAPTER XI

THE INTERACTION BETWEEN FORMAL AND INFORMAL STRUCTURE

The first task of life is to live. Man learns by the method of trial and error, but as soon as he becomes used to a certain way of doing things, he builds a mental superstructure around his activities and tries to transmit this superstructure in the form of beliefs, customs, habits, knowledge, law, etc. to the coming generations.

As every generation has to face new problems, there are always certain tensions between the realities of life and this mental superstructure, which needs constant readjustment, particularly in dynamic periods. Only relatively static cultures assume that their mental patterns suffice for all eventualities, and that there is no need for adjustment or innovation.

This relationship also exists in world society in which the superstructure embodies the results of past experience.

It is not only past experience which is mirrored in the superstructure of a society, but also its hierarchical structure. The experiences which are formalized and transmitted are those of the leading groups of a society, more than those of the rank and file.

The tensions between social reality in terms of "the flow of life" and the superstructure are caused by the two factors mentioned: the impact of the past in terms of a certain tendency to formalize the status quo and the impact of the most powerful states which determine the degree of efficacy of international organisations and of international law. The two factors are often intermingled: if the most powerful states adhere to a dynamic philosophy, they transmit those concepts also to world society, even if their national interests would be better served by stabilisation of the power structure than by changes. The stress on change often becomes either a verbal behavior form or it is applied mainly to changes which also serve national power interests.

The dominant interest in the preservation of the power structure as well as the fact that only limited national groups formulate foreign policy gives a higher degree of formalism to the superstructure of world society than to those of national societies. The internal policies of countries are the outcome of complex social processes in which many groups participate while this is much less true of foreign policy. The interests and emotions of most of the citizens are not directly reflected in the foreign policy of a country.

This may not be true in periods of extreme nationalism, but in those cases the nationalistic or expansionistic attitude is engineered by a small group which pursues more concrete goals compared to the vague nationalism of large masses. As long as a country is expansionistic, it is possible to keep nationalism at a high pitch because there is a general feeling that all will somehow share in the spoils or at least in the feeling of victory. If a country becomes satisfied with its place under the sun, it may take a certain pride in its cultural achievements but the "national emotion" will lose much of its intensity in most people, and at best persist as a vague feeling of cultural satisfaction, linguistic pride; a sense of history, of economic efficiency, of international status in terms of respect for "law and order," etc. Nationalism takes on the form of international respectability, analogous to the attitudes of the "better people" within national societies, who are disinclined to take heavy risks.

As the formal concepts of world society are generally formulated by countries which have acquired a sizeable amount of power and are not particularly anxious to advertise their desire for more power, the international philosophy tends to be conservative rather than radical. To acquire more than a reasonable amount of power is deemed to be most admirable and respectable; to speak of it is considered to be immature and vulgar and is regarded as an indication that a country wants too much and too soon. This is unwise and not at all respectable.

As the foreign policies of countries are generally formulated by the most respectable class of people, – the jobs are rather leisurely and involve travel –, there is a sort of cumulative effect of respectability in foreign relations which stands in strange contrast to the alarming crudeness of its reality of nuclear weapons, poison gas, bacteriological weapons, etc., etc.

One might feel tempted to formulate a psychological law: the more refined the superstructure, the cruder the reality. It would not be difficult to find striking illustrations of this "law" within many national societies. If the people within the national societies would take a greater and more direct interest in foreign policy, this might undoubtedly help to bring foreign policy to more normal proportions.

In the present time there is a noticeable lag between the mentality which is applied to foreign relations and that which is used in regard to internal relations.

While the latter in the modern industrial society uses the technique of reasoned compromise, foreign relations are approached with the mentality of power relationships of a primitive type because interstate relations take place no longer within the framework of a civilizational pattern but upon the basis of a power mentality which does not recognize the need for civilisational limitations, except those which the modern industrial society applies automatically out of a sense of self-preservation. There is perhaps an additional factor which leads to self-limitation because power is viewed through the spectacles of East and West. While they both accuse one another of striving for absolute power, they view their own power as aimed at the benefit of a fictitious individual, patterned after the ideas of the civilization of East or West.

It would undoubtedly be a considerable advantage if both East and West tried to view Man as he really is "hic et nunc," instead of imputing qualities and attributes to him which reflect our thinking about past situations rather than about the present time.

The reduction to the "minimal situation" which prevails in international affairs could perhaps be ameliorated if it were realized that the minimal interpretation of Man is an erroneous one. It only seems to possess reality if we apply it to abstractly conceived entities.

The individual as such cannot be seen as a power mechanism as he is always imbedded within a given social structure which causes a specific pattern of adaptation involving a restriction upon drives and impulses. The individual who thinks in terms of power thinks in terms of an out-group which he constructs as being different from his own group.

The use of the concept of "equality" in international relations would only possess reality if there were no social relations between the entities which are deemed to be "equal." In reality, any network of social relationships implies differentiation and inequality while the formal concept of equality can perhaps be regarded as a controlling device.

As such it means self-limitation, and it is exactly this concept of self-limitation which is not sufficiently developed in our international relationships. It stands in contrast to the idea of expansion which is innate in the economic thinking of Modern Man.

Unless this dichotomy can be in some way solved or at least put in a structural hierarchical relationship, there is little hope that the need for self-limitation will become the dominant principle of international relations. The existence of this principle in the formal superstructure is undoubtedly of significance, but it is not sufficient unless it also gains efficacy in regard to the internal situation of the most advanced countries.

The problem can also be seen in terms of interest groups: the interest groups which press for internal stability and the interest groups which strive for internal economic dynamism leading directly or indirectly to a certain internal expansionism. Although this situation could be measured to a certain extent by attitude tests, it seems safe to say that the majority of the populations of the major countries are unaware of this conflict of values and that the extremist groups on both sides are rather small. The power, however, behind the expansionistic groups is considerable because the goal of economic dynamism and of economic expansionism is an almost undisputed one which also finds little critical examination in the global sphere.

The need for self-limitation may be evident to certain intellectuals and to some religious and ethical groups, but they have but limited access to the mass media and only for formalized and therefore not very effective presentations of value patterns in which the relation of internal to external values is mostly omitted.

On the global level, the understandable and necessary dynamism of the less-developed countries obscures the need for self-limitation of power of the major countries and its relationships to economic goals. This configuration of factors leads to a kind of "as if philosophy," viz. "as if" economic dynamism and international stability are two motivations which can be reconciled without any great difficulty. This reconciliation might indeed be possible in terms of a sense of moderation, but it is exactly this moderation which is missing in the conflict areas of international relationships.

Moderation in this respect would imply a departure from a historically given situation to a projected state of affairs. This projection, however, is absent because no compromise seems possible between status quo and dynamic thinking, and both modes of thought seem equally unfair to the other party. The only possibility might lie in a moderate and regulated dynamism which would project concrete and limited solutions for brief but agreed-upon periods.

A fluid power policy would have to be the basis of such an attitude, and since power is more or less calculable, there is no reason why such a policy would not be possible upon an objective basis if increase and decrease of power were calculated for limited periods upon the basis of probability.

If such a policy were anchored in specific international organs, greater reality would be given to the global superstructure and this might lead to an evolutionary development of this superstructure which is very much needed. This evolutionary development can be reached sooner by the creation of additional, mostly functional organs than by trying to reform the existing superstructure without this added stimulus. The international superstructure is a social entity by itself: international organs influence other international organs. This form of communication is shorter than the path from national initiatives to international organs. This relationship is mostly in its most active form at the end of wars when national governments are in their most vulnerable period. This holds even true for victorious governments which have to cope with restive populations.

As soon as the relationship from national governments to international organs becomes static and overly formalized, the superstructure begins to show increasing lags in regard to social reality. This process has been most noticeable in the recent past, and it has led to a deterioration in the status of international organs. This is not the fault of those organs as such, but of the fact that they are too static to cope with the changes in the power structure of world society. It is a remnant of rationalism to assume that a static superstructure can deal with all possible variations in social reality.

A control system of world society would have to be linked to the innate controls which the modern industrial societies possess. There can never be any question of a coercive and centralised control as the mechanisms of world society are too complex for these outdated control mechanisms, while there is no trend towards centralisation in social reality. A control system which runs contrary to a mechanism can only wreck the mechanism: it is rather like trying to halt a car by shifting suddenly back to first gear.

One first has to know the workings of the mechanism before the controls can be devised.

In regard to world society, this means that the question has first to be put how the innate controls of this society work. The first control lies in the sense of self-preservation; the second one in the complexity of modern society, as this results in even minor disturbances perhaps having serious consequences.

The first control is not typical for our present world: all social groups, whether primitive or complex, have a sense of self-preservation. It could be argued, however, that this control is relatively weak in modern society because the complexity may cause mental fatigue and mental disturbances resulting in indifference.

The danger of a weakening of the "will to live" is very real in modern society but extremely difficult to analyze. It shows itself in certain attitudes of the younger generation and of deviant groups, which regard any form of complexity as their "mortal enemy."

It is often assumed that increasing prosperity and extended leisure will reduce the tensions which the complexity engenders. This might ultimately prove to be true, but we find ourselves in a transitional stage which is very hazardous. This hazard is increased because the complexity of modern society is carried beyond that needed for consumptive goals as world society strives for technical supremacy, rather than equality or cooperation. As there does not seem to be any technical superiority of one country over another for a prolonged period, the competitive tendency may eliminate itself and become transformed into real forms of coexistence and, ultimately, cooperation.

The complexity of modern society has had its origin in the mentality which was created by modern science and its thought systems. This complex mentality is dominant only in limited groups of our society while large segments of the population have retained a mentality which is more directly linked to emotional satisfaction. If modern society can engender emotional satisfaction in large population groups, this would in itself be a factor working towards stability.

It is extremely difficult to ascertain whether this emotional satisfaction exists in reality or whether emotions like fear, uncertainty, hatred, excessive tension, etc. play a dominant role. There is also no direct link between the attitudes of populations and the decision-makers in the field of foreign policy. Emotional stability would make political adventurism difficult; emotional instability, however, is subject to easy manipulation. Recent events in the field of international relations prove that the factor of emotional instability is still a factor of considerable importance. This is most evident in attitudes displayed towards the People's Republic of China as in this case one can find little that points towards a rational policy or one that shows a certain amount of foresight.

The controls which operate inside our societies do not operate in the direction of greater stability, and unless stability is made a dominant motive in the control system, there is much less likelihood of its development in international relations. The formalism of the latter field does not mean a striving for real stability as those behavior forms cover instability rather than stability. They are a compensatory mechanism instead of a control mechanism. Formal concepts as a compensatory device are a real danger because they offer no framework for the solution of conflict situations. It would be much better to recognize the conflict situations as such, and to aim for concrete solutions upon a compromise basis as we do within our societies, where verbal behavior forms reflecting a fictitious superstructure aimed at perfection are no longer used.

We need human solutions for human problems. It is an academic attitude to have great difficulty in viewing ourselves as humans. This may be true for the philosopher or the scientist who seeks the ultimate realities, but ninety-nine percent of mankind have simple answers to the question "What constitutes human well-being."

Reasonable need-satisfaction, a sense of "belonging" in small and tightly knit groups, stability, a set of values and beliefs, a certain artistic and ritual elaboration of the basic themes and stages of life would satisfy practically all human beings.

There are those who dream of mutation, and the emergence of a mental Superman. This is not likely as a reduction of tension would bring out the fundamental attributes of Man, which are now obscured by anxiety and fear and make him strive for goals of which the human values seem at least doubtful.

The goals which Man sets himself must be meaningful in terms of his human attributes and within a human content. Power for the sake of power whether this refers to power over nature or over man is not meaningful if it cannot be translated back into the values of permanence, stability and a reasonable relation between effort and result. It also involves a system of priorities, and an ordered and functioning world society deserves priority over any other goals which Man may set himself.

Without this goal, an uncontrolled chaos seems more likely than the world which Man might attain.

It seems wrong to present this world as a world of perfection as perfection is not a human attribute, at least not so far as groups are concerned and at best only in the case of a very few individuals. From world society we can expect no more than that it would be livable, reasonable and tolerant. If those are the goals, the means can be found by the control of population increase, by economic planning, by cultural freedom.

In terms of the individual this means a normal adjustment of means to ends, and a refusal to allow the means to play the role of goals. We have changed our means-systems, but our goal-systems cannot differ too much from those of stable and well-managed societies of the past.

To argue differently would mean the assumption of a basic change in Man himself. For this assumption there is no evidence.

The theories which assume the possibility of a "mutation" in Man seem to overlook that there was no mutation in the transition of simpler to more complex societies. This process can be explained by the fact of cumulative experience, which leads to better control over the social and natural environment.

The society of the future will see a much better control over the social environment, and a much wiser relationship between Man and Nature. This does not need a "mutation" but simply a more mature attitude, based upon Man's natural attributes which do not seem to undergo any significant change. A more mature society will undoubtedly not be interested in transferring Man at terrific costs to another planet where he can only survive under earth-simulated conditions. Man's habitat is the earth, and he is still a long way from creating an "earth society." Our societies so far have hovered between heaven and hell, with much closer proximity to the latter establishment.

To create a society which is adjusted to Man's nature as "he really is" constitutes a task to which we have not given ourselves wholeheartedly. It could be a simple task if we could overcome the mental artificiality which seems to rule our present world.

The future should mean the sense of freedom for which we all long.

CHAPTER XII

THE "CHANGE" FACTOR IN WORLD SOCIETY

It is just as unjustified to assert that Man does not change as to make "change" the dominant category of the processes of social evolution. If we regard Man as a part of nature, the process of evolution means growth. Growth is change within a given structural framework.

This growth is reflected in our consciousness but not in any simple or direct manner as our consciousness acts at all times in its totality in regard to our own organism and to the social and natural environment. In addition the structure of our consciousness is so complex that several ideas or images can exist in our mind at the same time.

If social growth results in an increase of experience, our mind must be able to process this experience. Experience is not an outer process, but an activity of the mind in relation to a "reality" which is only partially known to us. This "reality" we see as our own physical organism, the world outside us, other people, etc. but strangely enough we do not grant this attribute of reality to the processes of our mind itself. Yet the impressions, images, thoughts, ideas which occur in our mind are the only reality of which we are aware. The contents of our consciousness are at any given moment the only reality to us: a reality which is in constant motion, insecure, unstable so that we attempt to give it form by mental patterns and, ultimately, in verbal forms so that we can "communicate" a part of our "reality" to the "reality" of others, although those processes are far from distinct or accurate.

If I tell the physician that I feel a pain in my chest, he has only partial and incomplete information which he attempts to process via a system of knowledge which has been imparted to him as the result of generalized experience. If this generalized experience is made as complete and coherent as humanly possible, we talk about a "science" of this or that, and we are wont to believe that increased experience means more scientific behavior.

Experience cannot be regarded as any simple cumulative process: our mind reacts to impulses and, in order to gratify those impulses, it develops behavior patterns which activate a part of our experiences, but only that part which is relative to our impulses. In this sense, there is a certain continuity as we cannot assume that there have been very significant changes in the realm of impulses and needs although they may become more complex and more interlinked and interchangeable as Man matures.

Increased experience, however, also results in an increase in the size and structural complexity of our consciousness, and it is this factor which creates an overemphasized image of change which interprets change within the categories of greater complexity.

If a social group increases in complexity, interhuman pressures tend to increase. The increase of those pressures results in the projection of "change" as a desirable goal, often much beyond the degree to which the individual himself has additional or more complex impulses. Interhuman pressures force Man into a state of mental tension which projects another reality than that of the simpler or more natural person.

Experience in this sense becomes an even more complex process because it occurs on several mental levels. An intensified impulse, like the sex impulse in the life of the individual, may remain in the realm of direct physical desire; it may also stimulate the imagination or it may lead to mental efforts to find a way of gratifying the impulse.

In social groups, the mental patterns play a larger role than the direct emotional impulses which the group seeks to regulate for the sake of its own continuity. Because the group gathers and transmits experience mainly in mental patterns, it tends to accentuate experience in the mental form of knowledge.

In the individual, however, these mental patterns have to be related back to the realm of impulses and partially processed by the imagination. This means that social change tends to overshoot the mark and that there is a constant interplay between the mental patterns and the realm of emotions, which may resist, reject or be indifferent to the mental patterns, which then begin to lead an artificial life of their own which we only know too well in modern society and which accounts perhaps for the frightening superfluity and repetitiveness of much of our mental activities.

Social change seen in this way is a process of uncoordinated, chaotic and spontaneous social growth to which we impute all kinds of desirable attributes in order to make it palatable to the people who are forever doubtful whether these changes are meaningful in terms of their own need structure. Sometimes they are; mostly they are not because the nature-given fact that more people want more things has no significant impact on the emotional structure of the individual, except in the form of fear and anxiety that he may be left out where there are so many.

Social change in terms of the individual is dualistic: it creates resistance because greater complexity means greater effort; it causes pain and anxiety because it is difficult to find one's way through the web of a complex society; ultimately, the material results may offset some of the first reactions, but there is not often reason to present social change as a process which is pleasant to the individual.

This is in fact a propagandistic device employed by those who have to cope with more complex societies and who fear the alienation of the masses. These "leaders" may, however, tend to overlook the link between mental patterns and emotional substructures, and their edifices may become increasingly precarious by being built upon the sand of illusion instead of upon the rocks of emotional stability and satisfaction.

We would do better to talk of "progress pains" instead of creating a world of mental patterns, which are no more than empty and meaningless phrases to most people. This holds true also for patterns of knowledge, which are no longer emotionally meaningful to the individual.

The tension between the patterns of progress and emotional continuity causes a constant readjustment of those patterns unless objective natural factors heighten the speed of progress and enlarge the distance to such an extent that we can almost speak of "floating societies." These natural factors can take the form of excessive growth of population and the danger of diminishing resources.

These are exactly the factors which cause an excessive distance between mental patterns and emotional satisfaction.

Our "as if" society assumes the happiness of the individual while it suppresses the lingering suspicion about the reality of this assumption. The resulting "as if" happiness expresses the basic instability of our world.

While the mental structure is normally adjusted by the emotional current, this connection has become a-functional in our society. The stress upon "change" as a sort of moral supervalue is an indication of this, and the philosophers may again ponder over the explanation of this alarming cleavage between "Ought" and "Is," as the German thinkers of the nineteenth century used to do. Only they never hit upon the idea that the

"Ought" should be brought close to the "Is." Their intellectual reflection of Prussian militarism resulted in their sterile complaints about Man's inadequacy.

In the same vein the modern sociologist laments the lag between technology and culture, but he unfortunately reverses the terms. Technology is to him the "reality," while it is actually part of an artificial mental superstructure which should be contrasted with Man's emotional desire for stability and safety. The "culture" the sociologist often refers to are the social forms of a simpler period, and they persist perhaps because then the "Is" and "Ought" were closer together than they are in our period.

If the "Is" and "Ought" of modern society were brought closer together, our main concern would be with the stabilisation of the world's population and the adjustment of population to resources over a longer period. Both these essential tasks could be embodied in a meaningful "Ought pattern" which would possess significance to the individual because it would express his emotional concern with stability and security.

Our global superstructure neglects these problems completely but is dedicated to "change," although change in this respect very clearly means the aggravation of the problem rather than its solution.

As world society is in reality rudderless and leaderless, it is uneasily swayed by the emotions of frustrated masses. It is therefore not so amazing that it concentrates upon the most inhuman and most horrible tools of mass destruction ever conceived by Man.

It is entirely clear that this situation will not be improved by clamoring for the abolition of the tools, as this reverses the sequence of causation. Man's emotional instability and frustration are the causes of his inventing these disastrous tools. The tools themselves are hardly guilty as they are the expression of Man's perverted relationship to Nature.

It may look as if this leads to an utter condemnation of "change" as such. This is not the intention as what is condemned is only the adoration of "change" in the form of increasing the mental superstructure as a goal in itself, instead of seeing it as one attribute of Man's mind which stands in a structural relationship to the realm of his emotions as well as to that of his imagination.

Change may indeed be the expression of a lack of coordination in Man. If he were fully coordinated and adjusted, there would be no change but a stable individual and a stable society. This runs contrary to the concept of growth so that we may come to the conclusion that what our society needs is temperate and gradual change, taking its root in Man's natural impulses and desires as felt by him, but not as imputed to him.

It is evident that the changes which our society needs cannot be departmentalized and fragmentalized into the needs and aspirations of nations or the ambitions of sciences. The needs are universal: measured from the existing situation to a more desirable state of affairs, not in terms of conformity to mental patterns, but as a gradual and more complete unfolding of Man's innate capabilities.

The superstructure can never do this as these processes originate in the peoples. The superstructure can only project itself in such a way that it does not hinder Man's innate creativeness and that it establishes an "Ought" pattern which is meaningful in terms of Man's basic motivation.

The present superstructure of modern society petrifies and frustrates, and underneath it are the teeming, restless millions. Their frustrated emotions may mean aggression, apathy, rebellion, self-destruction. Once the frustration reaches a certain degree of intensity it will be set off by a spark, for which the push-button of the nuclear strategists has become the symbol. This is the expression of the magnitude and intensity of the frustration, and it is only because this frustration is so intense that we fail to realize what a terrible indication this symbol is. Or rather it portrays a situation that should fill us with utter alarm and with better notions than abolishing weapons or establishing a world government.

The superstructure is only meaningful in so far as it can be related back to the individual. It cannot ignore the identification of the individual with national groups in most cases, but this identification in the individual is rarely aggressive or expansionistic, unless it is engineered in this fashion. If the control groups of society do not exercise heavy pressures, the individual will seek an automatic balance unless the economic conditions make such a balance impossible.

This would lead us back to the problem of population in relation to resources as the dominant one of our times.

A science of international relations can have no other goal but to bring out the reality of things: a reality which is obscured by prejudices, artificial mental patterns and attempts to create complexity instead of simplicity.

The rules which the individual needs in order to live constructively in regard to his fellow-beings are basically simple and have been formulated many times by the leading civilisations and religions of our world. They are basically ethical rules which can gain effectiveness if certain basic requirements are met.

The individual cannot acquire mental balance if a certain physical equilibrium is not given. This fact is known to practically everybody, and it is quite possible to create the minimum requirements for this balance. We can only assume that Man is unable to reach a certain balance if we take a deterministic view of life, and this is exactly the mode of thought which has developed in the communist world as well as in the managerial democracies of the West, although perhaps to a lesser extent in the latter.

The dominant patterns are coercive instead of voluntarist, and this reduces Man to a mechanism, while he is a living creature. This artificiality creates the tensions which bring us every day closer to the brink of disaster. These patterns disguise themselves as a scientific view of life but science and its modes of thought rather stress than deny the voluntarist aspects of life. They form a system of probabilities which leaves us basically insecure and uncertain as our only solid foundation lies in our emotions, which determine the state of our happiness or unhappiness.

Emotional indifference is the widespread result of coercive patterns of living, and this indifference is a serious danger to the future of Mankind. To fight wars which are emotionally meaningless to those who are engaged in them is a form of emotional corruption whose practitioners will not hesitate to use the available means of total destruction. The very existence of these means themselves are already the expression of this emotional corruption.

"The modern weapons of war, and new concepts for using them, provide a brilliant illumination of Man's cleverness and the growing callousness of man to the welfare of his own race. Fire and blast have been man's ugly companions for uncounted years. But with the development of modern science new dimensions have been brought to these unwholesome familiars and some new companions have been added.

Nuclear weapons produce blast and fire on hitherto unimaginable scales. But they also supply a bonus in horror-radioactivity. Conventional poisons are now joined by the more subtle nerve gasses and the sickening agents of germ warfare. The capability for sheer savagery is now unbounded. Man's inhumanity to man can now reach unparalleled depths of horror." [1]

It would be wrong to attribute this "sheer savagery" to modern technology, but right to see a link between this savagery and the technological mentality.

[1] Thomas L. Martin and Donald C. Latham, Strategy for survival. Tucson, The University of Arizona Press, 1965.

This mentality seeks to dominate nature, but it neglects Man. It extends the concept of domination from nature to Man. The preceding centuries of poverty and the lust for power are at its roots so that it is unable to find its own measure.

A renewal of meaningful relationships between Man and Man provides the only possibility of re-establishing this measure. It means the transition from a mechanistic to a human measure in politics: compromise upon the basis of an equal right to live.

It is in this light that we have to understand the concept of change. It means change within the attributes of Man's structure: increased experience is not purely a mental process, but a widening of life's perspectives. A greater mastery, a certain "playfulness" as we move away from the sphere of power necessities.

Life is a theme with variations, and increased experience means that the variations become greater, more differentiated and more directly adjusted to the emotional structure of the individual. Man's psychic equipment is fully capable of countless variations, but this variety and differentiation has to come from within instead of being imposed from without. The coercive patterns which an overly complex society imposes tend to reduce Man's capability for growth although they must be regarded as a necessity in a period of transition.

What we lack, however, is the general perspective, the Mankind philosophy within which the concept of change can be placed in order to gain a relative value instead of an absolute one.

This is all the more clear if we apply the concept to the individual. To him change is never a goal in itself, but a means to an end. I change my surroundings, my tools, my job in order to make life more meaningful. Only a neurotic seeks change for the sake of change if there is no emotional necessity behind it. The anguish caused by uniformity and conformity may be a cause of changes which are irrational and catastrophic.

In addition, Man's consciousness seeks by its very nature a foundation in stable surroundings. If Man loves his town or his village, his home and his work, change is no longer meaningful. If he does not, he will seek to alter the conditions until they fit his requirements.

The normal person wishes stability unless he is motivated by the mental curiosity which is only a strong motive in some people.

These observations may seem trivial and conservative, but life seen in its continuity does not require a complex mentality, but rather a simple one. Mental complexity is a requirement of a complex society, but mental complexity can rest upon a simple and clear emotional structure. This structure is determined by the search for happiness which is always that of an individual, never of a group, because a group has no human identity.

Change may mean that Modern Man is in search of his identity, but it can never mean more than this. It is not the search for a social recipe, but a slow and gradual process of growth that can do no more than bring us the increased awareness, which is the most essential factor for our future.

CHAPTER XIII

ABOUT THE IMAGE OF THE FUTURE

Is Man really interested in the future? In his own future without any doubt, but only indirectly and vaguely in the future of the society in which he lives, unless this society is extremely dynamic so that its citizens are "engagés" to a great extent. In a more stable society, the individual vaguely thinks that things in the future will be pretty much what they are although he may consider it probable that Man will invent some more tools and some more ingenious gadgets.

The future is also not much the concern of the scientist: the natural sciences, apart from sciences like geology or biology, can free themselves from the time factor and occupy themselves with processes which can be repeated at any time and which mean a more or less permanent control over nature. History is concerned with the past, the humanities with patterns of permanence. The social scientist, envious of the success of the exact sciences, looks for recipes and magic formulas, but even he is not much concerned about the future although he has every reason to be. For him it would make his science more meaningful because it would give him an active stake in the world in which he lives. He shies away from the future because the future somehow would get him engaged in politics, and particularly in international politics, as national politics, considered as a separate entity, are no longer meaningful.

The future means a view of world society, a perspective on its potentialities although, of course, linked to and in terms of the evolution of national societies.

World society and national society involve the role structure of the individual. They mean that the individual can consider his role in regard to Mankind as a whole, in relation to his fellow nationals or both. He has no liberty in this respect as long as the national societies are strongly monopolistic and coercive and while world society has no direct link with the individual and cannot reach him. The reverse is also true: the individual cannot effectively reach world society, except perhaps in ethical terms which may bring him into conflict with the government of his own country. If a mankind attitude became more or less universal, governments would be powerless to cope with it, and this might be one of the ways in which a world society will become a reality, provided enough people grow tired of international conflicts which are often basically meaningless to them.

This is a process of gradual social evolution, which is stimulated by the emergence of the industrial society as the dominant social form. This society creates other forms of identification and allegiance than the national societies of the past although this process of evolution is hindered by the overlapping of both social forms in the case of large and powerful countries. It is indeed a strange but nevertheless justified conclusion that the processes of world society are retarded instead of aided by the most powerful countries, although their technical contributions may unwittingly help that decrease of their own power that is the conditio sine qua non for the emergence of a better coordinated world society.

The industrial society undoubtedly holds the stage as the most essential image of the future although its implications are perhaps not fully realized. It has developed in an antagonistic and competitive manner as it began within the social forms of the political society. If the forms of liberalism and democracy had been more widespread in the world, the industrial evolution might have been a gradual and even process. In reality it was most uneven because it took its origin in only a few countries which began to see it as a tool of political power.

In this way a dualism developed which made the political ideas of the West seem hypocritical to the rest of the world. While the political ideals were democratic and conciliatory, the economic dynamism was expansionistic and to the detriment of the poorer nations and the colonial peoples.

This increased the cleavage between the image of an egalitarian society and the reality of vast differences in wealth and power. In retrospect, it is not surprising that this dualism led to priority being given to economic goals under centralised governments in the form of communism. It was the only possible response to this dualism, which even within the Western world lead to the reassertion of the political society in terms of fascism and national-socialism.

This dualism has still not been overcome, and the welfare state is no more than an uneasy compromise between the industrial and the political societies. The vast bureaucracies of the modern welfare state utilize the power of the industrial society, but they pervert this power by limiting it to national groups, although in cases like those of Western Europe, the attempt is made to let the industrial society find its own social forms, although still – albeit fictitiously – in imitation of the social forms of the political society.

This fiction is neither a whole-hearted success, nor a complete failure. In the case of France, it has aroused the resistance of the political society, because supernationalism is unrealistic.

On the other hand, the forms of integration can be regarded as an attempt to create the social mechanisms which the industrial society needs, and in this respect they are most significant as a first step.

If it is realized that the industrial society has priority over the national political societies, the question arises whether it is essential to visualize the social forms which would be proper to this society.

This is a philosophical and sociological problem, but its elaboration and analysis could be a useful stimulus, as philosophical and social thinking often were in the past. This philosophical approach is largely lacking, but the attempt may nevertheless be made to formulate a few speculative remarks about this problem. When we speculated about the state, we approached its function and purpose in an abstract manner. We may do likewise for the industrial society.

While the purposes of the state were inner order and outer defense, the purposes of the industrial society cannot be defined in a similar manner.

The political society was originally not an integrative type of a society, but a structure which rested upon social and economic foundations which very much followed the dictates of their own growth. The state was not a total, but a restricted social form although, of course, there were the ideas of absolute power. However, these referred, at least initially, more to the form of state power than to an absolutism which we now visualize as totalitarianism.

Totalitarianism was the latter-day attempt to recreate the state after the image of the industrial society, but it failed because the political society is a society with limited functions.

The industrial society, on the other hand, is by nature an integrative type of society. It organizes life as a whole, and not in terms of limited exterior functions like order and defense.

Its principle of order is an inner, not an outer one, while its defense rests in its complexity and inviolability. For this reason it does not need outer coercive controls because it creates a much more immediate identification. The reason for this is perhaps that the goals of the industrial society aim more directly at the life-goals of the individual: the creation of material well-being, linked to a short working period which leaves ample time for recreation and leisure. One should add to this the factor of permanence, durability and harmony, but unfortunately this is not yet possible.

The industrial society is not seen as a specific social system in terms of the individual but as a society aiming at domination over both Nature and Man. This is the result of the remaining impact of the political society, as the domination of Man over Man is not meaningful in terms of the industrial society.

The industrial society is a cooperative social system, which consists of a highly complex role structure in which the individual has to fit himself upon the basis of a natural desire for activity, the realisation that a certain amount of work is necessary, and a certain amount of discipline, but not in terms of the military discipline of the political society.

The industrial society requires a mental discipline consisting of the adjustment to mechanical surroundings. This is different from the personal loyality required of the soldier.

The industrial society requires a mental discipline consisting of the
This frequently causes the feelings of isolation and lonesomeness which can, however, be adjusted at the small group level.

The great difficulty remains that the industrial society persists in regarding itself as a power mechanism and as an acquisitive type of society. This causes its lack of balance and its unnatural philosophy of continued expansion, which is definitely not meaningful in terms of the individual.

The individual on the other hand is too afraid and too uncertain to demand from the industrial society the permanence and stability which he really seeks. In this respect the industrial society is absolutist rather than democratic because the pattern of communication between producer and consumer is not a reciprocal relationship, but an influencing of masses by the technique of advertising, public relations and the mass media.

The revolt of the masses can only express itself in art, in apathy and indifference and in deviant forms of living which create unhappiness rather than happiness.

The democratisation of the industrial society is one of the most essential tasks of the future. It requires the organisation of the individual in his role of consumer as well as producer. While organisation is abundant in regard to the latter function, it is insufficiently developed in regard to the former. The mobilisation of the consumer would give the industrial society the much needed link between the control groups and the controlled. In this way, the industrial society could obtain the basis which would give it stability and which is lacking under present conditions. At present the control groups seek a continued increase of power, and this process has become one of looking continuously for new inventions.

Thus technology becomes the blind control mechanism of modern society, while a human measure is lacking. This measure could only be re-established by creating a natural link between the controllers and the controlled. To believe that this can be done by the outmoded mechanisms of the political society is entirely erroneous. They obscure reality, or at least, they do not lead to effective controls over the industrial society, as is most evident in the senseless production of a-functional armaments.

The needed limitation of the industrial society can only be achieved through the organisation of the masses in their role as consumers. If this were done in terms of functional groups, there would be an intermediary social form between the Western and the Communist worlds. One can visualize a council of producers and an assembly of consumers, alongside the existing political organizations and with a certain division of labor.

The egalitarian institutions of the West and the more functional ones of the communist world would be less antagonistic in regard to such organisations than they are at present towards each other.

The political ideas of the West must be adjusted to the industrial society before they can gain reality in the eyes of the peoples who feel little or no affinity for the traditional political parties.

The future should be seen in terms of concrete and realistic solutions of the problems of our present time, not as something new or fantastic. Man is an earth-bound creature, and his attitudes, beliefs, etc. are rooted in the need for survival. The only really essential change which is necessary is that we learn not to see "survival" as a problem of nations or blocs.

This is not a rational attitude as the interdependence of Mankind has already progressed so far that this attitude is no longer meaningful. The resources of the earth are the common possession of all nations, and each nation should use them as a trustee of world society.

This is already the attitude of many people all over the earth, but it is into the realm of business interests and national politics that this simple and self-evident truth does not seem to penetrate.

The permanence and continuity of life is given, but it is not the dominant factor in our philosophy. To see matters as they really are means seeing continuity and permanence, because our conflicts are too often about ephemeral things than about the essence of reality.

The reality is the wish for survival of more than 3000 million people, who are in this respect our equals. Modern society constructs itself automatically upon this basis, but this should remain constantly in our minds. It is the idea which can become the starting-point for a more elaborate and concrete pattern of global thinking.

The future of Mankind is not a matter of organisation, but a matter of feeling and thought. Above all it is a matter of simple and concrete thinking, motivated by the feeling of a common destiny.

BIBLIOGRAPHY

AARON (R. I.); P. A. REYNOLDS, "Peaceful coexistence and peaceful co-operation," *Polit. Stud.* (Oxford) 4(3), Oct. 56: 283–296.

APPADORAI (A.), *The use of force in international relations.* Bombay, Asia Publishing House, 58, 124 p.

ARON (R.), *Paix et guerre entre les nations.* Paris, Calmann-Lévy, 62, 797 p. CR: *R. int. Sci. soc.* 14(4), 1962: 825–827; J.-B. DUROSELLE, *R. franç. Sci. polit.* 12(4), déc. 62: 963–979.

ARON (R), "Une sociologie des relations internationales," *R. franç. Sociol.* 4(3), juil.-sept. 63: 307320.

BIE (P.) de, "Contenidos de conciencia, estructuras y relaciones internacionales" (Contents of consciousness, structures and international relations), *R. Estud. politic.* 108, Nov.-Dec. 59: 87–108.

BIE (P.) de, "Sociologische facetten der internationale samenwerking" [Sociological facets of international co-operation], *Mens en Mij.* 34(I) 59: 2–17.

BOULDING (K. E.), *Conflict and defense: a general theory.* New York, Harper and Brothers, 62, IX + 349 p. CR: J. S. HARSANYI, *Amer. econ. R.* 53(4), Sept. 62: 903–904; C. A. MCCLELLAND, *J. Conflict Resol.* 6(I), Mar. 62: 88–95.

BOURGEOIS (L.), "La morale internationale." *Revue générale de droit int. public,* XXIX, 1922, p. 5–22.

BOURQUIN (M.), L'Etat souverain et l'organisation internationale; l'organisation internationale et l'enquête de la Dotation Carnegie. Préparé pour la Dotation Carnegie pour la paix internationale. New York, Manhattan Publishing Co., 59. 237 p.

BOURQUIN (M.), *Stabilité et mouvement dans l'ordre juridique internationale.* Paris (Recueil Sirey) 1939. 131 pag. Académie de droit intern., *Recueil des cours,* 64 (1938, II), p. 347–477.

BRIERLY (J. L.), "The function of law in international relations." *Problems of Peace,* 3rd series, August 1928, London 1929, p. 278–298.

BURTON (J. W.), *International relations. A general theory.* Cambridge, The Univ. Press. 1965.

BURTON (J. W.), "Peace research and international relations," *J. Conflict Resol.* 8 (3), Sept. 64: 281–286.

CARR (EDWARD H.), *Twenty years crisis.* London, Macmillan & co. Ltd. 1962.

CLAUDE (T. L.), *Power and international relations.* New York, Random House 1965.

CONFERENCE ON TENSIONS IN DEVELOPMENT. Oxford University, 1961. *Restless nations; a study of world tensions and development.* New York, Dodd, Mead, 62, 217 p.

CONSTANTOPOULOS (D.), "Les raisons de la crise du droit de la guerre," *Jb. int. Recht.* 7(1), 57: 22–33.

CORBETT (P. E.), "Law and society in the relations of states." *The Year Book of World Affairs,* [IV], 1950, p. 23–53.

[ĐORDEVIĆ] DJORDJEVIĆ (J.), "Philosophical and sociological bases of co-existence," *Ind. for Aff.* I (1), Jan. 58: 20–26.

ETHICAL *values in international decision-making*, the conference of June, 16–20, 1958. By B. Landheer, G. van der Molen (etc.) The Hague, Nijhoff 1960. 80. 103 p. (Stichting Grotius Seminarium).

EVAN (W. M.); M. A. SCHWARTZ, "Law and the emergence of formal organization," *Sociol. soc. Rel.* 48(3), April 64: 270–280.

FOCSANEANU (L.), "Le 'leadership' dans la communauté internationale," *Annu. A. A. A.* 30, 1960: 122–148.

FRAGA IRIBARNE (M.), *La guerra y la teoría del conflicto social* (War and the theory of social conflict). Madrid, Real Academia de Ciencias Morales y Políticas, 62, 160 p. CR: E. MANERA, *R. Polít. int.* (Madrid) 61, May-June 62: 237–241.

FRIEDMANN (W.), *Law in a changing society.* Berkeley, Univ. of Calif. Press, 59, 522 p.

FRIEDMANN (W. G.), "Sociology of law," *Curr. Sociol.* 10–11(I), 1961–1962: 1–34. [A trend report and bibliography.]

GARCÍA ARIAS (L.), *La guerra moderna y la organización internacional* (Modern war and international organization). Madrid, Instituto de Estudios políticos, 62, 590 p. CR: C. BARCIA TRELLES, *R. Polít. int.* (Madrid) 67, May-June 63: 209–211.

GROSS (F.), "La sociologie des relations internationales. Etudes et recherches," *R. int. Sci. soc.* 12(2), 60: 295–303.

GUGGENHEIM (PAUL), "Die soziologischen Grundlagen des Völkerrechts." *Die Friedens-Warte*, XXIX, 1929, p. 38–41.

GUGGENHEIM (PAUL), "International Relations and Public International Law." *Geneva special studies*, XI, No. 2, 1940, p. 7–19.

GURVITCH (GEORGES), "La philosophie du droit de Hugo Grotius et la théorie moderne du droit international." *Revue de métaphysique et de morale*, Paris 1925, p. 365–391.

GURVITCH (GEORGES), "Problèmes de la sociologie du droit", in: G. Gurvitch, *Traité de Sociologie*. Tome II. Paris, Presses univ. de France, 58: 173–206.

HART (W. A.), 't. *Psychologie der internationale betrekkingen* (Psychology of int. relations) Utrecht, Oosthoek, 57, VI + 207 p.

HAZARD (JOHN N.), "The Soviet Union and International Law." *Soviet studies*, I, No. 3, 1950, p. 189–199.

HAMIDULLAH (MUHAMMAD), *Muslim Conduct of State*. Being a treatise of Muslim public international law, consisting of the laws of peace, war and neutrality, together with precedents from orthodox practice, and preceded by a historical and general introduction. [Revised edition.] Lahore (Ashraf) 1945. XV. 352 pag. [Ière édition anglaise en 1941].

VAN HEEK (F.), "The sociological aspects of war," *Int. J. comp. Sociol.* 5(1) Mar. 64: 25–39.

HOFFMANN (STANLEY), (Editor) *Contemporary theory in international relations.* Eaglewood Cliffs N. J. Prentice Hall, Inc. June 1965.

HUBER (MAX), "Beiträge zur Kenntnis der soziologischen Grundlagen des Völkerrechts und der Staatengesellschaft." *Jahrbuch des öffentl. Rechts der Gegenwart*, IV, 1910, p. 56–134.

HUBER (MAX), *Die gerechtlichen Grundlagen des heutigen Völkerrechts.* [Vermischte Schriften, III:] Gesellschaft und Humanität, Zürich (Atlantis) 1948, p. 177–196.

HUBER (MAX), *Die soziologischen Grundlagen des Völkerrechts.* Berlin-Grünewald (Rothschild) 1928. VII, 101 pag.

KAPLAN (M. A.), *Some problems in the strategic analysis of international politics.* Princeton, N. J., Center of International Studies, Woodrow Wilson School of Public and International Affairs, Princeton University, 59. 37 p.

Kaplan (Morton A.), and Nicholas de B. Katzenbach, *The political foundations of international law*. New York-London, 1961.

Keeton (George W.), and G. Schwarzenberger, *Making International Law Work*. 2nd edition. London, Stevens & sons 1946. Z, 266 pag.

Kelsen (H.), "Naturrechtslehre und Rechtspositivismus" (natural law theory and legal positivism), *Polit. Vjhschr.* 3(4), Dec. 62: 316–325. With discussion by V. D. Gablentz: 325–327, and by H. Guradze, *ibid.* 4(2), June 63: 196–199.

Kelsen (H.), *What is justice? Justice, law and politics in the mirror of science; collected essays*. Berkeley, Calif. Univ. of Cal. Press, 57, 397 p.

Kelsen (Hans), "What is the Reason for the Validity of Law?" *Grundprobleme des Intern. Rechts, Festschrift f. Jean Spiropoulos*, Bonn, 1957, p. 257–263.

Klineberg (O.), *The human dimension in international relations*. New York, Holt, Rinehart and Winston, 64 VIII + 173 p. CR: M. A. Kaplan, *Amer. pol. Sci. R.* 58 (3) Sept. 64: 682–683.

Korovine (E.), "La République des Soviets et le droit international." *Revue générale de droit int. public*, XXXII, 1925, p. 292–312.

Kraus (Herbert), "La morale internationale." Paris (Hachette) 1928. 154 pag. Académie de droit intern. *Recueil des cours*, 16 (1927, I), p. 385–539.

Krylov (Serge), *Les notions principales du droit des gens*. (La doctrine soviétique du droit international.) Paris (Recueil Sirey) 1948. 70 pag.

Landheer (B.), "Die Struktur der Weltgesellschaft und ihre rechtliche Formgebung." Tübingen 1964. 13 p. Sonderdruck aus *Archiv des Völkerrechts*, XII, 1 (Oktober 1964).

Landheer (B.), "The concept and determination of national power." *Int. Spectator*, 8 dec. 1955 (9, n. 23), p. 761–771.

Landheer (B.), "State-mobility as a sociological concept." *Internationales Recht und Diplomatie*, 1960 (1), p. 53–62.

Landheer (B.), "Sociological theory and international law." Texte d'une conférence devant le VIe Congrès annuel de l'A.A.A. en mai 1954 à Sarrebruck. *Annales Universitatis Saraviensis*, 1954, no. 3/4, p. 180–191.

Landheer (B.), "Possibilities and method of a peace science." *Reconciliation quarterly*, 1963 (n. 120), p. 333–335.

Landheer (B.), "Interstate competition and survival potential." *The journal of conflict resolution*, June 1959 (3, n. 2), p. 162–171.

Landheer (B.), *Beeld van de Toekomst*. Rotterdam, Lemniscaat 1965.

Landheer (B.), De sociologische benadering *van internationale problemen*. Rede uitgesproken bij de aanvaarding van het ambt van bijzonder hoogleraar aan de Rijksuniversiteit te Groningen op dinsdag 20 maart 1962. 's-Gravenhage, Nijhoff 1962, 8o. 24 p.

Landheer (B.), Pause *for transition. An analysis of the relations of man, mind and society*. The Hague, Nijhoff, 1957. 8o. VII, 284 p.

Landheer (B.), Mind and Society. *Epistemological essays on sociology*. The Hague, Nijhoff, 1952. 8o. 112 p.

Landheer (B.), "Remarks on a Structural Approach to International Relations and its Influence on International Law." *Grundprobleme des Intern. Rechts, Festschrift f. Jean Spiropoulos*, Bonn 1957, p. 307–320.

Landheer (B.), "Sociological Theory and International Law." *Annales Universitatis Saraviensis*, 1954. No. 3/4, p. 180–191

Landheer (B.), "Sociological Aspects of European Integration." *Annuaire européen/European Yearbook*, III, The Hague, Nijhoff 1957, p. 53–69.

Laun (Rudolf), *Der Wandel der Ideen Staat und Volk als Äusserung des Weltgewissens*. Barcelona (Imp. Elzeviriana) 1933. XXX, 463 pag.

Lauterpacht (H.), "The Law of Nations, the Law of Nature and the Rights of Man."

(Read before the Grotius society on 7th Dec. 1942), *Transactions of the Grotius society*, XXIX, 1944, p. 1–33.

LEVI (W.), "On the causes of peace," *J. Conflict. Res.* 8 (1), Mar. 64: 23–35.

MCDOUGAL (M. S.); F. P. FELICIANO, The initiation of coercion: a multitemporal analysis," *Am. Int. Law* 52(2), Apr. 58: 241–259.

MACKAY (M. C. J.), "Agressiviteit en oorlog" (Aggressiveness and war), *Int. Spectator* 16(19), Nov. 62: 510–530.

MACKAY (M. C. J.), "Ethische waarden in de internationale politiek" (Ethical values in international politics), *Int. Spectator* 14(21), 8 Dec. 60: 539–652.

MELVIN (B. E.); A. T. ARAIM, "La sociología de las relaciones internacionales" (The sociology of international relations), *R. mexic. Sociol.* 18(I), Jan.-Apr. 56: 113–124.

VAN DER MOLEN (G. H. J.), "De 'onderontwikkelde' landen en het recht" (Underdeveloped countries and law) *Mens en Mij.* 35 (5) Sept-Oct. 1960: 377–388.

MORGENTHAU (HANS J.), *Politics among the nations* 3rd. ed. New York, Alfred A. Knopf 1965.

NIEMEYER (GERHART), *Law Without Force. The function of politics in international law.* Princeton, Princeton university press. London, Milford 1941. XIV, 408 pag.

NORTHROP (F. S. C.), "Naturalistic and Cultural Foundations for a more Effective International Law." *The Yale law journal*, LIX, No. 8, 1950, p. 1430–1450.

PEN (J.), "Réflexions sur les théories du conflit," *Cah. ISÉA* 132, déc. 62 (Sér. M. no. 15): 37–56.

POUND (ROSCOE), "Philosophical Theory and International Law." *Biblioteca Visseriana*, I, Lugduni Batavorum (Brill) 1923, p. 71–90.

PROBLEME der Einigung Europas. (Europäische Wochen in Hamburg). [Contributions de Rudolf Laun, B. Landheer, etc.) Düsseldorf, Gebr. Hermes 1960]. 80. [XIII,], 226 p. (*Schriftenreihe zur europ. Integration*, Organ des Europa-Kolleges in Hamburg, 1.)

PRUITT (D. G.), "An analysis of responsiveness between nations," *J. Conflict Resol.* 6(I), Mar. 62: 5–18.

RAESTAD (ARNOLD), *La philosophie du droit international public.* (Oeuvre posthume. Préface par M. Raestad.) Oslo, Dybwad 1949. 117 pag.

REEVES (JESSE S.), "International Society and International Law." *American journal of int. law*, XV, No. 3, 1921, p. 361–374.

REHBINDER (M.), "Entwicklung und gegenwärtiger Stand der rechtssoziologischen Literatur" (Development and actual state of juridico-sociological literature), *Kölner Z. Soziol. soz.-Psychol.* 16(3), 1964: 533–567.

RÖLING (B. V. A.), *International Law in an Expanded World.* Amsterdam, Djambatan 1960.

ROUCEK (J. S.), "La sociología de la guerra y de la organización internacional" [Sociology of war and of international organization], *R. mexic. Sociol.* 20(I) Jan.-Apr. 58: 181–208.

SCELLE (GEORGES), "Le concept de société internationale: ses conséquences en technique juridique." *Revue de droit int.*, XV, No. 1, 1935, p. 7–35.

SCHINDLER (D.), "Übergangsformen zwischen Krieg und Frieden" (Forms of transition between war and peace), *Schweiz. Mh.* 40(2), May 60: 113–125.

SIMPSON (J. L.); H. FOX, *International arbitration: law and practice.* Published under the auspices of the David Davies Memorial Institute of International Studies. New York, Praeger-London, Stevens & Sons, 59. 330 p.

SINGER (J. D.), "International conflict: three levels of analysis," *Wld. Polit.* 12(3) Apr. 60: 453–465.

SNYDER (R. C.), "Some recent trends in international relations theory," in: A. RANNEY (ed.) *Essays on the behavioral study of politics.* Urbana, University of Illinois Press, 62: 103–172.

SCHELER (H.), *Der Marxismus über den imperialistischen Krieg in unserer Epoche* (Marxism on imperialistic war in our era). Berlin, Dietz, 57, 283 p.

SCHLESINGER (R.) "Co-existence as a framework of social evolution," *Coexistence* I, May 64: 46–53.

SCHINDLER (DIETRICH), "Contribution à l'étude des facteurs sociologiques et psychologiques du droit international." Paris (Recueil Sirey), 1934, 98 pag. Académie de droit intern., *Recueil des cours*, 46 (1933, IV), p. 299–326.

SCHOCH (J.), *Der soziologische und tiefenpsychologische Aspekt des Krieges* (The sociological and depth-psychological aspect of war). Zürich, O. FÜSSLI, 55, 99 p.

SCHWARZENBERGER (GEORG), "International Law and Society." *The Year Book of world affairs*, (I) 1947, p. 159–177.

SCHWARZENBERGER (GEORG), "Jus pacis ac belli? Prolegomena to a sociology of international law." *American journal of int. law*, XXXVII, No. 3, 1943, p. 460–479.

SCHWARZENBERGER (GEORG),"The Inter-disciplinary Treatment of International Law." *Grundprobleme des Intern. Rechts, Festschrift f. Jean Spiropoulos*, Bonn, 1957, p. 401–409.

SNYDER (RICHARD C.), H. W. BRUCK and BURTON SAPIN, *Decision-making as an approach to the Study of International Politics*. Princeton University, Organizational behavior section, June 1954.

STONE (JULIUS), "Of Sociological Inquiries Concerning International Law." *Grundprobleme des Intern. Rechts, Festschrift f. Jean Spiropoulos*, Bonn, 1957, p. 411–423.

STRACHEY (A.), *The unconscious motives of war; a psycho-analytical contribution*. London, Allen & Unwin; New York, Int. Univ. Press, 57, 283 p.

TRUYOL Y SERRA (A.), *La teoría de las relaciones internacionales como sociología* (The theory of international relations as sociology). 2nd rev. ed. Madrid, Instituto de Estudios políticos, 63, 65 p. CR: A. LINEARES, *R. Polít. int.* (Madrid) 69, Sept.-Oct. 63: 283–284.

VALKENBURGH (P.), "Naar een sociologische theorie van de oorlog" (Towards a sociological theory of war), *Sociol. Gids* 9(4), 1962: 178–192.

VECCHIO (G.), del. *Persona, estado y derecho* (Person, State and law) Preface by Man. Fraga Iribarne, Madrid, Instituto de Estudios Políticos, 57, 582 p.

VERDROSS (ALFRED), "Die gesellschaftswissenschaftlichen Grundlagen der Völkerrechtstheorie." *Archiv f. Rechts- und Wirtschaftsphilosophie*, XVIII, No. 3, 1925, p. 413–431.

VLEKKE (B. H. M.), "Quelques aspects théoriques de l'étude des relations internationales," *Polit. étr.* 27(3), 1962: 230–245.

WIESE (L.), VON; HONINGSHEIM, P. *Kriegssoziologie* (Sociology of war) Stuttgart, Fischer, 58, 8 p.

WOLFERS (ARNOLD), *Discord and collaboration*. Baltimore, The Johns Hopkins Press, 1962.

WRIGHT (Q.), "Toward a universal law for mankind," *Columbia Law. R.* 63(3), Mar. 63: 435–459.

WRIGHT (QUINCY), The study of international relations. New York, Appleton-Century, Crofts, Inc. 1955.

WRIGHT (QUINCY), "Design for a research project on international conflicts and the factors causing their aggravation or amelioration," *West. polit. Quart.* 10(2) June 57: 263–275.

WRIGHT (QUINCY), "The peaceful adjustment of international relations: problems and research approaches," *J. soc. Issues* II (I), 55: 3: 12.

YAKEMTCHOUK (R.), "Droit des gens positif et sociologie des relations internationales," *R. Inst. Sociol.* (2), 58 335–390.

GPSR Compliance

The European Union's (EU) General Product Safety Regulation (GPSR) is a set of rules that requires consumer products to be safe and our obligations to ensure this.

If you have any concerns about our products, you can contact us on ProductSafety@springernature.com

In case Publisher is established outside the EU, the EU authorized representative is:

Springer Nature Customer Service Center GmbH
Europaplatz 3
69115 Heidelberg, Germany

Batch number: 10830943

Printed by Printforce, the Netherlands